D0930021

At Issue

Poverty in America

Other Books in the At Issue Series:

At Issue

Poverty in America

Tamara Thompson, Book Editor

GREENHAVEN PRESS
A part of Gale, Cengage Learning

GALE
CENGAGE Learning·

Farmington Hills, Mich • San Francisco • New York • Waterville, Maine
Meriden, Conn • Mason, Ohio • Chicago

Patricia Coryell, *Vice President & Publisher, New Products & GVRL*
Douglas Dentino, *Manager, New Products*
Judy Galens, *Acquisitions Editor*

For more information, contact:
Greenhaven Press
27500 Drake Rd.
Farmington Hills, MI 48331-3535
Or you can visit our Internet site at gale.cengage.com

For product information and technology assistance, contact us at

Gale Customer Support, 1-800-877-4253
For permission to use material from this text or product, submit all requests online at www.cengage.com/permissions.

Further permissions questions can be e-mailed to permissionrequest@cengage.com.

Articles in Greenhaven Press anthologies are often edited for length to meet page requirements. In addition, original titles of these works are changed to clearly present the main thesis and to explicitly indicate the author's opinion. Every effort is made to ensure that Greenhaven Press accurately reflects the original intent of the authors. Every effort has been made to trace the owners of copyrighted material.

Cover photograph copyright © Images.com/Corbis.

LIBRARY OF CONGRESS CATALOGING-IN-PUBLICATION DATA

Poverty in America / Tamara Thompson, book editor.
        pages cm. -- (At issue)
    Includes bibliographical references and index.
    ISBN 978-0-7377-7183-1 (hardcover) -- ISBN 978-0-7377-7184-8 (pbk.)
    1. Poverty--United States. 2. United States--Economic conditions. 3. United States--Social conditions. I. Thompson, Tamara.
    HC110.P6P5966 2015
    362.50973--dc23
                                                                            2014044391

Printed in Mexico
1 2 3 4 5 6 7 19 18 17 16 15

Contents

Introduction

According to statistics from the US Census Bureau, every fifth student who picks up this book lives in poverty, meaning income in their household falls below the federal poverty level ($23,834 for a family of four in 2013). Roughly 20 percent of American children under the age of eighteen experienced poverty in 2013, while some 45.3 million Americans (14.5 percent of the population) were living at or below the federal poverty threshold.

At the most extreme end, the National Poverty Center estimates that more than 1.65 million households lived in "extreme poverty"—surviving on $2 or less per person, per day—during any given month in 2011.

Poverty has long been one of America's most intractable and challenging problems, spurring President Lyndon B. Johnson to famously declare "an unconditional war on poverty" in 1964 and vow that although it wouldn't be easy, "we shall not rest until that war is won."[1]

Fifty years after Johnson's declaration, that war has not been won. Although the programs of Johnson's "Great Society"—such as food stamps, the Medicare and Medicaid health insurance programs, and the Economic Opportunity Act—helped millions avoid or escape poverty, more recent political policy shifts have, for better or worse, fundamentally changed the way the country helps its poor. Meanwhile, economic conditions have fundamentally changed both the demographics and the depth of poverty in America.

Fueled by a subprime mortgage-lending crisis and excessive leverage at many of the country's largest banks, the 2007–2009 Great Recession was the biggest US economic contraction since the Great Depression. Although the recession

---

1. Lyndon B. Johnson "State of the Union (January 8, 1964)," Miller Center, accessed September 28, 2014. http://millercenter.org/president/speeches/speech-3382.

officially ended more than five years ago, its effects are still reverberating throughout the economy, as evidenced by a so-called jobless recovery and economic growth that continues to be sluggish.

The Great Recession rearranged the US economic landscape and widened the already-yawning income gap between rich and poor, but it also did something else: it brought poverty to the suburban bastion of the middle class.

According to researchers from the Brookings Institution, "America's major suburbs have become home to the largest and fastest-growing poor population in the country. Between 2000 and 2011, the number of poor residents in suburbia grew by almost two-thirds, or 64 percent—more than double the pace of poverty growth in the large cities that anchor these regions. For the first time, more poor people in America live in suburbs than in big cities."[2]

The new suburban poor have had a very different economic experience from the poor who live in historically impoverished inner cities or rural areas with persistent and/or generational poverty, such as the Deep South or Appalachia regions.

"The tale of the newly poor . . . is the narrative of millions of Americans who had economic security, enjoyed something of the comforts of an affluent society, and then lost it," writes Sasha Abramsky in his book *The American Way of Poverty: How the Other Half Still Lives.* "Not since the Great Depression," Abramsky continues, "have so many millions of people been so thoroughly beaten down by vast, destructive forces."[3]

Those "vast, destructive forces" include a stubbornly high unemployment rate, the proliferation of low-wage work, the decline of American manufacturing and industry, the out-

2. Alan Berube and Elizabeth Kneebone, "America's Shifting Suburban Battlegrounds," Brookings Institution, August 16, 2013. www.brookings.edu/research/opinions/2013/08/16-suburban-poverty-berube-kneebone.
3. Sasha Abramsky, *The American Way of Poverty: How the Other Half Still Lives.* New York: Nation, 2013.

sourcing of jobs overseas, growing income inequality, and a brutal economic crisis that devastated the middle class.

"Financial hardship in America is described in terms of a 'struggling middle class,'" note Kristin S. Seefeldt and John D. Graham in their 2013 book *America's Poor and the Great Recession*. "The irony of that characterization is that what the middle class is struggling against—and what portions of it have now fallen into—is poverty."[4]

Since suburban areas have historically been economically stable, there are scant social services in place to aid the millions of suburban families who have slipped down the economic ladder.

An additional difficulty is that the welfare reforms enacted by President Bill Clinton in 1996 ended the only cash entitlement program for poor families with children (Aid to Families with Dependent Children, or AFDC) and replaced it with a program called Temporary Assistance for Needy Families (TANF), which requires recipients to work in order to receive cash assistance for a lifetime maximum of five years per family.

Yet with such a deep and long-lasting recession, many Americans—both middle class and not—have found themselves shut out of the workforce for extended periods of time, sometimes for years on end.

Almost all government aid for the poor (TANF, housing subsidies, and the Earned Income Tax Credit, for example) is reserved for people who are actively working. Individuals who are not currently participating in the workforce—the very people who needed help most during the recession—are essentially cut off from public benefits.

Although the Clinton-era welfare reforms are widely credited with shrinking America's welfare rolls and getting millions to join or rejoin the workforce, the number of Ameri-

4. Kristin S. Seefeldt and John D. Graham, *America's Poor and the Great Recession*. Bloomington: Indiana University Press, 2013.

cans living in extreme poverty—on $2 a day or less—has grown "dramatically" over the past two decades, according to H. Luke Shaefer and Kathryn Edin, from 1.7 percent of all households in 1996 to 4.3 percent in 2011, making it the fastest-growing poverty segment.[5]

The only government help such a desperately impoverished person can get if they don't have a job is from the Supplemental Nutrition Assistance Program (SNAP, formerly known as food stamps). Research by the *New York Times* found that an estimated six million Americans who earn no cash income or receive other aid rely exclusively on SNAP benefits to survive; they are the poorest of the country's poor.[6]

In response to the Great Recession, President Barack Obama bolstered the social safety net in 2009 by extending eligibility for unemployment insurance and increasing SNAP benefits across the board. Those benefits were later eliminated by congressional Republicans, who argued that providing resources to the poor and unemployed was the wrong way to promote economic stimulus and recovery.

The authors in *At Issue: Poverty in America* present a wide range of viewpoints about the causes and effects of poverty, whether and under what circumstances the government should provide assistance to the poor, and whether being "poor" by American standards of living qualifies as poverty at all.

5. H. Luke Shaefer and Kathryn Edin, "Rising Extreme Poverty in the United States and the Response of Federal Means-Tested Transfer Programs," National Poverty Center, May 2013. http://npc.umich.edu/publications/u/2013-06-npc-working-paper.pdf.
6. Jason Deparle and Robert M. Gebeloff, "Living on Nothing but Food Stamps," *New York Times*, January 2, 2010. www.nytimes.com/2010/01/03/us/03foodstamps.html?pagewanted=all.

Overview:
America's War on Poverty

John Halpin and Karl Agne

John Halpin is a senior fellow at the Center for American Progress, a nonpartisan research and educational institute. Karl Agne is a founding partner of GBA Strategies, a public opinion research and communications firm.

The country has made significant economic and social strides since President Lyndon B. Johnson famously declared an "unconditional War on Poverty" in 1964, but despite improvements in many areas, poverty remains deeply entrenched in American society. Today, up to a third of all Americans experience economic hardship and an estimated 39 percent live at or below the federal poverty level. Most people believe that poverty is the result of systemic failures, such as a bad economy or misguided public policies on jobs and education, rather than the fault of poor people themselves. Individuals across the political spectrum agree the government has a responsibility to do more to combat the problem of poverty in America.

Fifty years ago, President Lyndon B. Johnson declared an "unconditional War on Poverty" in his State of the Union address on January 8, 1964. The War on Poverty created a number of important federal and state initiatives that remain in place today—from Head Start [a government health and

John Halpin and Karl Agne, "50 Years After LBJ's War on Poverty: A Study of American Attitudes About Work, Economic Opportunity, and the Social Safety Net," Center for American Progress, January 7, 2014.

education program for low-income children] to nutrition assistance to Medicare and Medicaid [the government's health insurance programs for seniors and the poor.]. These initiatives, coupled with the civil rights advances of the era and the overall strong economy in the 1960s, led to a reduction in the number of people living in poverty from around 19 percent to a historic low of 11.1 percent by the early 1970s.

President Johnson described his War on Poverty as a continuation of the basic American bargain that all people should be given a decent shot at achieving their life goals and securing stable lives built on genuine freedom and economic opportunity:

> This budget, and this year's legislative program, are designed to help each and every American citizen fulfill his basic hopes—his hopes for a fair chance to make good; his hopes for fair play from the law; his hopes for a full-time job on full-time pay; his hopes for a decent home for his family in a decent community; his hopes for a good school for his children with good teachers; and his hopes for security when faced with sickness or unemployment or old age.

One-quarter to one-third of Americans—and even higher percentages of Millennials and people of color—continue to experience direct economic hardship.

Since the start of the War on Poverty, however, much has changed in our society and our economy; some developments are positive and some negative. Women, people of color, the elderly, and people with disabilities are more strongly protected by law and more integrated into parts of our society and economy than they were in the 1960s. At the same time, many people continue to suffer from ongoing discrimination at work and in terms of wages. What's more, economic opportunities, such as decent-paying jobs, a secure retirement, affordable health care, and education, have diminished for many

Americans in the bottom end of the income distribution as income and wealth have taken off for those at the very top. The financial crisis of 2007–2008 and the subsequent Great Recession further highlighted the breakdown of the U.S. economy and the ongoing struggle many people face finding employment, decent wages, and secure and supportive communities for raising and educating their children.

About the Report

With this context, we set out to determine what Americans know and believe about poverty and assess their retrospective opinions about the War on Poverty itself and their support or opposition to new proposals for righting poverty in the future. This report includes results from focus groups and a major survey of more than 2,000 American adults, including significant oversamples of Millennials, African Americans, and Latinos, to assess attitudes among these important constituencies.

The most important findings from the research include:

• *One-quarter to one-third of Americans—and even higher percentages of Millennials and people of color—continue to experience direct economic hardship.*

Sixty-one percent of Americans say their family's income is falling behind the cost of living, compared to just 8 percent who feel they are getting ahead and 29 percent who feel they are staying even. Twenty-five percent to 34 percent of Americans report serious problems falling behind in rent, mortgage, or utilities payments or being unable to buy enough food, afford necessary medical care, or keep up with minimum credit card payments. While these numbers have somewhat retreated over the past five years, they are still shockingly high, and the disparities across demographic groups underscore how uneven the current recovery has been.

• *A majority of Americans have a direct personal connection to poverty.*

Fifty-four percent of Americans say that someone in their immediate or extended families is poor, a figure that has actually increased 2 percentage points since we conducted our first poll in 2008. Nearly two in three African Americans (65 percent) report a direct connection to poverty, while 59 percent of Hispanics say the same.

• *Americans vastly overestimate the annual income necessary to be officially considered poor.*

Today, with unemployment closer to pre-financial crisis levels and a recovery ostensibly underway for several years, government statistics tell us that 15 percent of Americans live below the poverty level.

Estimates of Poverty

Perhaps expressing a more realistic understanding of the economy than official government measures currently capture, Americans on average estimate that it takes just more than $30,000 in annual income for a family of four to be considered officially in poverty—about $7,000 more than the government's poverty line of $23,550 for a household of four. Most respondents in the focus groups were shocked to hear that the official poverty line was as low as it is; many suggested that it represents a disconnect with the reality of rising prices over the past few years. Americans on average also report that it would take more than $55,000 in annual income to be considered out of poverty and safely in the middle class.

• *Americans now believe that nearly 40 percent of their fellow citizens are living in poverty.*

When we conducted our 2008 poll, 13.2 percent of Americans were living below the federal poverty line, but our survey found that Americans guessed the number to be 29 percent. Today, with unemployment closer to pre-financial crisis levels and a recovery ostensibly underway for several years, government statistics tell us that 15 percent of Americans live below the poverty level. The public, however, believes that number is now 39 percent—a stunning 10-percentage-point increase that flies in the face of economic indicators such as the unemployment rate, consumer confidence, the financial markets, and gross domestic product, or GDP.

• *Americans strongly believe that poverty is primarily the result of a failed economy rather than the result of personal decisions and lack of effort.*

The public is clear about its priorities for reducing poverty: jobs, wages, and education.

Economics and Idealism

In a forced choice test of ideas, nearly two in three Americans (64 percent) agree more with a structural argument about the causes of poverty. A majority agree that "Most people who live in poverty are poor because their jobs don't pay enough, they lack good health care and education, and things cost too much for them to save and get ahead," underscoring the current economy's failings in the areas of wages, health care, education, and cost of living. In contrast, only 25 percent of Americans agree more with a personal cause: "Most people who live in poverty are poor because they make bad decisions or act irresponsibly in their own lives." Even white conservatives and libertarians prefer the structural vision of a failed economy to personal reasons for poverty by a wide margin of 63 percent to 29 percent, respectively.

• *Retrospective evaluations of the War on Poverty are mixed, but Americans across ideological and partisan lines believe the government has a responsibility to use its resources to fight poverty.*

Americans do not generally have a favorable impression of the term "the War on Poverty" without additional context about the programs and goals associated with the larger project. But after introducing information to describe the War on Poverty and its impact, an overwhelming percentage of Americans—86 percent—agrees that the government has a responsibility to use some of its resources to combat poverty. Moreover, a majority (61 percent) feels that the War on Poverty has made a difference—albeit not a major difference—in achieving its goals; 41 percent say the War on Poverty has made a minor difference; and 20 percent say it has made a major difference. Retrospective evaluations of the War on Poverty, however, are heavily divided by ideology, partisanship, and race. Nearly 7 in 10 (69 percent) white liberals and progressives believe the War on Poverty has worked, and more than 6 in 10 (64 percent) white conservatives and libertarians believe the opposite.

• *Despite mixed feelings about the original War on Poverty, there is strong support for a more realistic goal of reducing poverty by half over the next 10 years.*

Realistic Goals

Asked whether they would support or oppose "the president and Congress setting a national goal to cut poverty in the United States in half within 10 years," 7 in 10 Americans said they would support such a goal—40 percent of the public would *strongly* support the goal—and only 22 percent would oppose it. This figure is quite similar to the 74 percent support reported in the first study in 2008. Support for a national goal of cutting poverty in half is very strong among African Americans (87 percent support and 58 percent strongly support) and reaches roughly 80 percent among both Millennials (79 percent) and Latinos (79 percent). Sixty-five percent of whites support this goal, as do a majority of Democrats (89 percent), independents (66 percent), and Republicans (54 percent).

• *The public is clear about its priorities for reducing poverty: jobs, wages, and education.*

Asked which two areas they believe are most important for new investments, 40 percent of Americans choose creating jobs and increasing wages; 30 percent choose job training and workplace preparation; 25 percent choose elementary and secondary education; 23 percent choose college access and affordability; and 21 percent choose early childhood education.

• *Americans also express very strong support for a number of policies to help reduce poverty rates with particular intensity around jobs, wages, and education but also on more traditional safety net items.*

Policy Proposals

Of the 11 policy ideas tested, five proposals received 80 percent or higher total support and 50 percent or higher strong support from Americans. These five policy proposals are: help low-wage workers afford quality child care (86 percent total support and 52 percent strong support); expand nutrition assistance to provide families with healthy food and enough to eat (85 percent total support and 50 percent strong support); make universal pre-kindergarten available for all children (84 percent total support and 59 percent strong support); expand publicly funded scholarships to help more families afford college (84 percent total support and 54 percent strong support); and increase the minimum wage and make sure it rises with inflation (80 percent total support and 58 percent strong support). A second tier of anti-poverty proposals includes ideas for expanded tax credits such as the Earned Income Tax Credit, or EITC, Child Tax Credit, and access to affordable health coverage, as well as proposals for a new national jobs program and more refinancing of mortgages. Roughly three-quarters of those polled support these proposals, and more than 40 percent strongly support them.

Public Support

Policymakers should feel confident that the American public will support efforts to expand economic opportunity, increase access to good jobs and wages, and maintain a robust social safety net. Harsh negative attitudes about the poor that seemingly defined political discussions throughout the 1980s and 1990s have given way to public recognition that many Americans—poor and middle class alike—are facing many pressures trying to stay afloat and get ahead in the difficult economic environment. Supporters of anti-poverty efforts should not be complacent in their efforts, however, and should recognize that although Americans back government action to reduce poverty, questions remain about the structure and scope of these efforts and how effective they have been over time.

A Variety of Factors Contribute to Poverty

Ron Haskins

Ron Haskins is a former White House and congressional advisor on welfare issues who was instrumental in the 1996 overhaul of national welfare policy. He currently codirects the Brookings Center on Children and Families.

Poverty is a complex issue with no single cause, but there are several known contributing factors. One of the biggest factors in child poverty, for example, is the prevalence of single-parent households headed by women, who are far less likely to participate in the workforce than men. Both women and men show declining work rates, however, and wages that have not kept up with inflation are another critical issue. Whether or not someone has a college education is also a major predictor of poverty, and the fact that minorities lag far behind their white peers in access to higher education is of special concern. Similarly, poor education and low skills among immigrants are the main drivers of high poverty rates in those populations.

Few topics have enjoyed as much attention from federal policymakers over the past half century as poverty and what can be done to reduce it. . . .

After some initial progress in the 1960s, and continuing progress for the elderly, the nation has made surprisingly little progress against poverty. The nation's inability to reduce children's poverty is especially troublesome. A review of the leading causes of poverty shows why trends in the economy, demography, and education make progress against poverty so difficult to achieve.

In the United States, with the important exception of those on Social Security, the only way for most adults and families to avoid poverty is to work. Yet between 1980 and 2009, work rates for men declined from 74.2 percent to 67.6 percent, a fall of around 9 percent. The trend for young black men (ages 20–24) is even worse. Starting from the very low base of 60.9 percent, their ratio declined to the startling level of 46.9 percent, a decline of nearly 23 percent. Work among young black males is a national crisis.

[The] uneven record of maintaining high levels of work is a leading cause of poverty in America.

The work rate of women stands in sharp contrast to that of men. In 2007 before the Great Recession set in, 58.1 percent of women were working, a 25 percent increase since 1980. These figures reflect the post-World War II trend of the relentlessly increasing participation by women—including mothers of young children—in the nation's economy. Equally impressive is the 20 percent rise in work by lone mothers over the same period, a trend that bears directly on child poverty rates because children in female-headed families are four or five times (depending on the year) more likely to be in poverty than children in married-couple families.

Women Lag in the Workforce

Even more important for the nation's poverty rate, work by never-married mothers rose more sharply than that of any other group during the 1990s. These mothers and their children have always been the group most likely to be in poverty, including long-term poverty, in large part because their work rates have been so low. In 1983, for example, only about only 35 percent of never-married mothers worked. After the welfare reform legislation of 1996, their work rate exploded, increasing from 46.5 percent in 1995 to 66.0 percent in 1999, an increase of more than 40 percent in just four years. Equally surprising, after a lengthy period of employment stagnation and decline associated with the mild recession of 2001 and the deep recession of 2007–2009, in 2010 their work rate was still more than 25 percent higher than it had been before welfare reform in the mid-1990s.

The fact that in 2007—before the Great Recession—the work rates of males and females were 72 percent and 58 percent respectively, combined with the fact that the poverty rate for individuals in families in which no one works is nearly eight times as high as the poverty rate for individuals in families with at least one full-time, year-round worker, shows that there is plenty of room for improvement. This uneven record of maintaining high levels of work is a leading cause of poverty in America. Without high work levels, it will be difficult to mount an effective fight against poverty.

Wages Are Stagnant

Wage rates are a second work-associated factor that has a major impact on poverty. Based on data from the U.S. Census Bureau, trends in wages since 1979 can be succinctly summarized. Wages at the 10th percentile fell and then recovered and ended the nearly three decade period almost exactly where they were in 1979. The general trend of wages at the 50th percentile was a slow increase amounting to about a 10 percent rise over the entire period. At the top, by contrast, wages did very well, increasing 32 percent over the period at the 90th percentile. If we were to plot wages higher up in the distribution, they would rise even higher.

In 2007, wages at the 10th percentile were about $8 per hour, more or less where they were in 1979 if inflation is taken into account. Working at this wage for 35 hours a week year round, a person would earn $14,560, $2,145 under the poverty level for a family of three. It is an amazing mathematical fact that 10 percent of all workers will always be at the 10th percentile of earnings or below. Thus, if wages do not improve at the bottom, all single parents with two or more children at or below the 10th percentile—and even many above the 10th percentile—will always be in poverty if earnings are their only income.

Without a college degree, 45 percent of the children from families in the bottom fifth of income will themselves be mired in the bottom fifth as adults.

Family Composition

In 2009, the poverty rate for children in married-couple families was 11.0 percent. By contrast, the poverty rate for children in female-headed families was 44.3 percent. The difference between these two poverty rates is a specter haunting American social policy because the percentage of American children who live in female-headed families has been increasing relentlessly for over five decades. In 1950, 6.3 percent of families with children were headed by a single mother. By 2010, 23.9 percent of families with children had single-mother heads. That a higher and higher fraction of children live in the family type in which they are about four times as likely to be poor exerts strong upward pressure on the poverty rate. One way to think of the shift to female-headed families is that even if government policy were successful in moving people out of poverty, the large changes in family composition serve to offset at least part of the progress that otherwise would be made.

In fact, a Brookings analysis shows that if we had the marriage rate we had in 1970, the poverty rate would fall by more than 25 percent.

The U.S. now seems to be mired in a situation in which the nation's young people are at a level of educational achievement that is inferior to that of young people from many other nations.

Education Plays an Important Role

There now appears to be universal agreement that the combination of technological advances and globalization have resulted in education being a major factor in determining the employment and earnings of many American workers. Census Bureau data on the relationship between education and family income since the 1960s show that families headed by adults with more education make more money. Some of the differences are huge. In 2009, the difference in median family income between families headed by an individual who dropped out of high school and families headed by an individual with a bachelor's degree or higher was about $68,600 ($31,100 compared with $99,700). Even more pertinent for examining the causes of poverty, family income for those with less than a college degree has been stagnant or declining for three decades. Without a college degree, 45 percent of the children from families in the bottom fifth of income will themselves be mired in the bottom fifth as adults. By contrast, with a college degree, adult children cut their odds of staying in the bottom fifth all the way down to 16 percent from 45 percent. The odds of making it to the top quintiles indicate similar abrupt changes if youngsters from poor families manage to achieve a college degree.

Despite the great advantages of having a college degree, James Heckman has demonstrated that the high school graduation rate reached its highest level at about 80 percent in the late 1960s and has since decreased by 4 to 5 percentage points. A high school degree is usually required for college admission. Moreover, a significant gap remains between the graduation rate of white students (above 80 percent) and black and Hispanic students (both about 65 percent). Ethnic gaps such as these are a continuing plague on the nation's social policy.

A Discouraging Picture

The four-year college enrollment and graduation rates of students from families with varying levels of income renders the education picture discouraging. Youngsters from higher-income families are more likely both to enroll in and graduate from college than youngsters from poorer families. For example, 79 percent of children whose parents were in the top income [quintile] enrolled in college and 53 percent earned a four-year degree. But only 34 percent of children whose parents were in the bottom income quintile enrolled in college and only 11 percent received a four-year degree. If education is one of the routes out of poverty, the American educational system seems to be perpetuating poverty and income distinctions as much as it facilitates movement up the income scale.

The effectiveness of the nation's K-12 education system is cast into serious doubt by comparing the performance of U.S. students with students from other OECD [Organisation for Economic Co-operation and Development] nations. In the most recent version of the Program for International Student Assessment (PISA), the U.S. was tied with two other countries for 27th in math, was 17th in science, and tied for 12th in reading. A recent volume by Claudia Golden and Lawrence Katz of Harvard presents a strong case that past U.S. achievements in international competitiveness were due in large part to the superiority of the nation's system of universal education and excellent colleges and universities. The U.S. now seems to be mired in a situation in which the nation's young people are at a level of educational achievement that is inferior to that of young people from many other nations. Thus, not only will the modest educational achievement of many Americans continue to make progress against poverty difficult, but American competitiveness in the global economy seems threatened.

Immigration Is a Factor

Until the recent recession, America had been experiencing one of the greatest waves of immigration in its history. For the past two decades, an average of about one million immigrants has obtained legal permanent resident status in the U.S. each year. In addition, according to the Pew Hispanic Center, in the seven years before the Great Recession, the population of un-documented immigrants grew by an average of a little over 500,000 per year. In a nation that prides itself on being built by immigrants, these large numbers alone are not particularly daunting. However, as George Borjas of Harvard shows, about 20 percent of immigrants have less than a 9th grade education as compared with a little less than 3 percent of non-immigrants. Consistent with the relatively large number of immigrants who lack even minimally adequate education, Borjas also finds a long-term trend toward lower wages among immigrants. In 1940, the age-adjusted average wage of first-generation male immigrants was 5.8 percent above the average wage of non-immigrant males. This figure fell to 1.4 percent above the average wage of non-immigrant males in 1970 and then dropped dramatically to 20 percent below the non-immigrant male wage in 2000.

It comes as little surprise, then, that the poverty rate among immigrants is higher than the poverty rate among native-born Americans. In 2009, the immigrant poverty rate was 19.0 percent as compared with 13.7 percent for native-born Americans. Given that the overall poverty rate for the nation was 14.3 percent, the poverty rate would be lower by about 0.6 percentage points (or around 1.9 million people) if the immigrant poverty rate were the same as the poverty rate for native-born citizens.

The Causes of Poverty Remain Strong

Reflecting on these five major causes of poverty leads one to understand why it has been so hard for the U.S. to make much progress against poverty despite the proliferation of social programs and the substantial increases in spending . . . since President Johnson first declared war on poverty in the mid-1960s. Declining work rates, stagnant wages, the rise of female-headed families, inferior education, and the arrival of millions of immigrants with poor education and low skills are little engines pushing up the poverty rate. Conditions in the U.S. virtually ensure high poverty rates because the underlying factors that cause poverty have remained very strong.

Many Who Experience Poverty Are the "Working Poor"

Hope Yen

Hope Yen is a Washington, DC-based national reporter for the Associated Press, a news wire service.

For the first time in US history, the majority of households receiving food stamps—a key indicator of poverty—consist of working-age people who are typically employed for low wages. Full- and part-time workers who are employed year-round experienced the greatest increase in food stamp use since 1980, according to a recent analysis of government data. Increasingly, such individuals are college-educated and formerly part of the middle class. Analysts say the recent economic recession played an instrumental role in the demographic shift, along with broader economic factors such as high unemployment, the decline of American manufacturing, stagnant wages, income inequality, globalization, and the outsourcing of American jobs overseas.

In a first, working-age people now make up the majority in U.S. households that rely on food stamps—a switch from a few years ago, when children and the elderly were the main recipients.

Some of the change is due to demographics, such as the trend toward having fewer children. But a slow economic recovery with high unemployment, stagnant wages and an increasing gulf between low-wage and high-skill jobs also plays a big role. It suggests that government spending on the $80 billion-a-year food stamp program—twice what it cost five years ago—may not subside significantly anytime soon.

Food stamp participation since 1980 has grown the fastest among workers with some college training, a sign that the safety net has stretched further to cover America's former middle class, according to an analysis of government data for The Associated Press [AP] by economists at the University of Kentucky. Formally called Supplemental Nutrition Assistance, or SNAP, the program now covers 1 in 7 Americans.

The findings coincide with the latest economic data showing workers' wages and salaries growing at the lowest rate relative to corporate profits in U.S. history.

A low-wage job supplemented with food stamps is becoming more common for the working poor.

President Barack Obama's State of the Union address Tuesday night [January 28, 2014] is expected to focus in part on reducing income inequality, such as by raising the federal minimum wage. Congress, meanwhile, is debating cuts to food stamps, with Republicans including House Majority Leader Eric Cantor, R-Va., wanting a $4 billion-a-year reduction to an anti-poverty program that they say promotes dependency and abuse.

The Plight of the Working Poor

Economists say having a job may no longer be enough for self-sufficiency in today's economy.

"A low-wage job supplemented with food stamps is becoming more common for the working poor," said Timothy Smeeding, an economics professor at the University of Wisconsin-Madison who specializes in income inequality. "Many of the U.S. jobs now being created are low- or minimum-wage—part-time or in areas such as retail or fast food—which means food stamp use will stay high for some time, even after unemployment improves."

The newer food stamp recipients include Maggie Barcellano, 25, of Austin, Texas. A high school graduate, she enrolled in college but didn't complete her nursing degree after she could no longer afford the tuition.

Hoping to boost her credentials, she went through emergency medical technician training with the Army National Guard last year but was unable to find work as a paramedic because of the additional certification and fees required. Barcellano, now the mother of a 3-year-old daughter, finally took a job as a home health aide, working six days a week at $10 an hour. Struggling with the low income, she recently applied for food stamps with the help of the nonprofit Any Baby Can, to help save up for paramedic training.

"It's devastating," Barcellano said. "When I left for the Army I was so motivated, thinking I was creating a situation where I could give my daughter what I know she deserves. But when I came back and basically found myself in the same situation, it was like it was all for naught."

Since 2009, more than 50 percent of U.S. households receiving food stamps have been adults ages 18 to 59, according to the Census Bureau's Current Population Survey. The food stamp program defines non-elderly adults as anyone younger than 60.

Many good-paying jobs in areas such as manufacturing have disappeared, shrinking the American middle class and bumping people with higher levels of education into lower-wage work.

As recently as 1998, the working-age share of food stamp households was at a low of 44 percent, before the dot-com bust and subsequent recessions in 2001 and 2007 pushed new enrollees into the program, according to the analysis by James Ziliak, director of the Center for Poverty Research at the University of Kentucky.

The Demographics of Food Stamps

By education, about 28 percent of food stamp households are headed by a person with at least some college training, up from 8 percent in 1980. Among those with four-year college degrees, the share rose from 3 percent to 7 percent. High-school graduates head the bulk of food stamp households at 37 percent, up from 28 percent. In contrast, food stamp households headed by a high-school dropout have dropped by more than half, to 28 percent.

The shifts in food stamp participation come amid broader changes to the economy such as automation, globalization and outsourcing, which have polarized the job market. Many good-paying jobs in areas such as manufacturing have disappeared, shrinking the American middle class and bumping people with higher levels of education into lower-wage work.

An analysis Ziliak conducted for the AP finds that stagnant wages and income inequality play an increasing role in the growth of food stamp rolls.

Taking into account changing family structure, higher unemployment and policy expansions to the food stamp program, the analysis shows that stagnant wages and income inequality explained just 3.5 percent of the change in food stamp enrollment from 1980 to 2011. But from 2000 to 2011, wages and inequality accounted for 13 percent of the increase.

What the Future Holds

Several economists say food stamp rolls are likely to remain elevated for some time. Historically, there has been a lag before an improving unemployment rate leads to a substantial decline in food stamp rolls; the Congressional Budget Office has projected it could take 10 years.

"We do not expect income inequality stabilizing or declining in the absence of real wage growth or a significant reduction in unemployment and underemployment problems," said Ishwar Khatiwada, an economist for the Center for Labor Market Studies at Northeastern University who reviewed the Labor and Commerce departments' wage data.

Full- and part-time workers employed year-round saw the fastest growth in food stamp participation since 1980, making up 17 percent and 7 percent of households, respectively. In contrast, the share of food stamp households headed by an unemployed person has remained largely unchanged, at 53 percent. Part-year workers declined in food stamp share.

4

Child Poverty
Is a Critical Problem

Marian Wright Edelman

Marian Wright Edelman is president and founder of the Children's Defense Fund, a national child advocacy and research organization.

The number of American children living in poverty is staggering. More than fifteen million children are poor, and more than one in five will experience poverty during the most crucial years of brain development. Children are the largest group of Americans experiencing poverty, and younger children and children of color are far more likely to be impoverished. Importantly, childhood poverty has long-term negative effects, with poor children having more health problems, greater high school dropout rates, increased criminality, and greater economic insecurity as adults. But childhood poverty is not a permanent condition and can be ended if we make a real commitment to do so. Only by ending childhood poverty can we provide children a level playing field on which to grow.

Just released US Census Bureau data reveal 45.3 million people were poor in America in 2013. One in three of those who are poor is a child. Children remain our poorest age group and children of color and those under five are the poorest. More than one in five infants, toddlers, and pre-schoolers were poor during their years of greatest brain development and vulnerability. Black children saw no decrease and continue to have the highest child poverty rates in the nation. In 20 states more than 40 percent of Black children were poor and nearly one in five Black children were living in extreme poverty with an annual income of less than half of the poverty level or $33 a day for a family of four.

Although the percentage of poor children dropped in 2013 for the first time since 2000, from 21.8 percent (16.1 million) in 2012 to 19.9 percent (14.7 million), there were still 1.3 million more poor children than in 2007 before the recession began.

It is a moral disgrace that child poverty in the United States is higher than adult poverty, higher than for children in almost all other competitor nations, and higher than our country with the world's largest economy should ever allow. Wealth and income inequality are still at record high levels and opportunity gaps are widening. What values and priorities do these unjust realities reflect? Isn't it time to reset our moral and economic compass? If we want to build a strong workforce, military, and economy and ensure the most basic tenets of opportunity for the most vulnerable, we must and can end child poverty now.

Child poverty has huge economic costs for the nation. Year after year the lost productivity and extra health and criminal justice costs associated with it add up to roughly half a trillion dollars.

Poverty in Childhood Creates Long-Term Negative Effects

Poverty hurts children and destroys their dreams, hopes, and opportunities. Poor children are more likely to go hungry, which is associated with lower reading and math scores, greater physical and mental health problems, higher incidence of emotional and behavioral problems, and a greater chance of obesity. Poor children are less likely to have access to affordable quality health coverage, have more severe health problems, and fare worse than higher income children with the same problems. A poor child with asthma is more likely to be reported in poor health, spend more days in bed, and have more hospital episodes than a high-income child with asthma. Poor children suffer a 30 million word interaction gap by age 3 and are less likely to enter school ready to learn and to graduate from high school. One study found children who were poor for half of their childhood were nearly 90 percent more likely to enter their 20s without completing high school than never-poor children.

Child poverty increases the risk of unemployment and economic hardship in adulthood. Those who experienced poverty at any point during their childhood were more than three times as likely to be poor at age 30 as those who were never poor as children. The longer a child is poor, the greater the risk of poverty in adulthood and experiencing poverty as a child also increases the likelihood of lifelong health problems and involvement in the criminal justice system. Child poverty scars some children for life.

Child poverty has huge economic costs for the nation. Year after year the lost productivity and extra health and criminal justice costs associated with it add up to roughly half a trillion dollars, or 3.8 percent of our nation's gross domestic product (GDP). What we can never measure though are the countless innovations and discoveries and contributions that did not occur for our nation because children's potentials were stunted by poverty.

Poverty Is a Result of Choices Made

It does not have to be this way. Child poverty is not an act of God. It is the choices of men and women and we can change it. Child poverty can be ended and prevented if we want to.

Poverty rates change over time with the economy and with changes in government policies. The United States has made substantial progress in reducing poverty over the past 50 years despite worsening inequality and increased unemployment. Child poverty dropped 36 percent between 1967 and 2012 when income from tax credits and in-kind benefits like nutrition and housing assistance are counted. Ending child poverty would save lives and money and increase productivity. For example, eliminating child poverty between the prenatal years and age 5 would increase lifetime earnings between $53,000 and $100,000 per child, for a total lifetime benefit of $20 to $36 billion for children born in a given year. When are we going to gain enough moral, common and economic sense to treat our children justly and give all of them a level playing field upon which to grow? Children have only one childhood and it is today. Chilean Nobel laureate Gabriela Mistral said, "We are guilty of many errors and many faults, but our worst crime is abandoning the children, neglecting the fountain of life. Many of the things we need can wait. The child cannot. Right now is the time his bones are being formed, his blood is being made, and his senses are being developed. To him we cannot answer 'Tomorrow.' His name is today."

Given that the United States has been blessed with great wealth and high ideals which we need to live up to and given the high costs we incur from child poverty every year, how can our country not act to end child poverty now?

5

Poverty Impacts Rural Communities

US Department of Agriculture

The US Department of Agriculture is the federal agency responsible for developing and enacting government policies on farming, agriculture, forestry, and food.

While poverty is present in both American cities and rural communities, "nonmetro" areas nationwide experience more poverty overall. Statistics vary from state to state, region to region, and even from county to county within regions, but areas with the most severe poverty include the historically poor rural areas of the southeast, the Mississippi Delta, the Appalachia region, and Native American lands. Many of these communities are "persistently poor," meaning the majority of the population has lived in poverty for the past thirty years. Higher rates of poverty are also now appearing in rural areas of the southwest, northwest, Pacific, and northeast due to de-industrialization, increased immigration, and the so-called Great Recession.

In the United States, people living in poverty tend to be clustered in certain regions, counties, and neighborhoods rather than being spread evenly across the Nation. Research has shown that the poor living in areas where poverty is prevalent face impediments beyond those of their individual circumstances. Concentrated poverty contributes to poor housing and health conditions, higher crime and school dropout rates, as well as employment dislocations. As a result, economic conditions in very poor areas can create limited opportunities for poor residents that become self-perpetuating.

While the overall rate of nonmetro poverty is higher than metro poverty, the difference in nonmetro and metro poverty rates varies significantly across regions. The nonmetro and metro poverty rate gap for the South has historically been the largest, averaging 5.1 percentage points over the last two decades. In 2012, the South had a nonmetro poverty rate of 22.1 percent—nearly 7 percentage points higher than in the region's metro areas. The difference in poverty rates in the South is particularly important for the overall nonmetro poverty rate because an estimated 43.1 percent of the nonmetro population lived in this region in 2012. Regional poverty rates for nonmetro and metro areas were most alike in the Midwest and the Northeast in 2012.

There are currently 353 persistently poor counties in the United States (comprising 11.2 percent of all U.S. counties).

County-Level Poverty

The American Community Survey (ACS) was developed by the Census Bureau to replace the long form of the decennial census. It uses a rolling sample of housing units (250,000 monthly) to provide basic population characteristics annually for areas with populations of 65,000 or more. ACS accumulates samples over 3- and 5-year intervals to produce estimates for areas with smaller populations; only the 5-year average ACS provides coverage for all counties in the nation. The 2008–12 ACS is used here to examine poverty at the county level.

Counties with a high incidence of poverty are mainly concentrated in the South. Those with the most severe poverty are found in historically poor areas of the Southeast, including the Mississippi Delta and Appalachia, as well as on Native American lands. Pockets of high poverty are increasingly found in other regions, such as nonmetro areas of the Southwest and the North Central Midwest. The incidence of poverty is relatively low elsewhere, but in general higher rates of poverty are found in the Midwest, Southwest, Pacific, and Northeast than in the past. Deindustrialization since the 1980s contributed to the spread of poverty in the Midwest and the Northeast. Another factor was rapid growth in Hispanic populations, which tend to be poorer, particularly in California, Nevada, Arizona, Colorado, North Carolina, and Georgia over the 1990s and 2000s. Finally, the poverty impact of the 2007–09 recession was fairly widespread.

Persistence of Poverty

An important dimension of poverty is time. An area that has a high level of poverty this year, but not next year, is likely better off than an area that has a high level of poverty in both years. To shed light on this aspect of poverty, ERS [the US Department of Agriculture's Economic Research Service] has defined counties as being persistently poor if 20 percent or more of their populations were living in poverty over the last 30 years (measured by the 1980, 1990 and 2000 decennial censuses and 2007–11 American Community Survey 5-year estimates). Using this definition, there are currently 353 persistently poor counties in the United States (comprising 11.2 percent of all U.S. counties). The large majority (301 or 85.3 percent) of the persistent-poverty counties are nonmetro, accounting for 15.2 percent of all nonmetro counties. Persistent poverty also demonstrates a strong regional pattern, with nearly 84 percent of persistent-poverty counties in the South, comprising of more than 20 percent of all counties in the region.

Degree of Rurality and Proximity to Urban Cores

Metro counties are commonly characterized as densely populated central cities and suburbs, and nonmetro counties as sparsely populated small towns and open countryside. This distinction oversimplifies the many differences across metro and nonmetro areas. Some metro counties have relatively small populations and are adjacent to rural areas, and some nonmetro counties contain urban areas but still qualify as nonmetro. A more comprehensive classification—separating metro areas into highly and less-urbanized counties (using metro area population as cutoffs) and categorizing nonmetro areas by degree of urbanization and adjacency to metro areas—reveals important differences in poverty. For instance, this classification indicates that degree of poverty and degree of rurality are linked. More than 35 percent of the people living in completely rural counties live in high-poverty counties and more than 26 percent live in persistent-poverty counties. In contrast, about 6 percent of the people living in the most urban nonmetro areas live in high-poverty counties and 4 percent live in persistent-poverty counties.

6

A First-Hand Account of Living in Poverty

Jenn

Jenn is a real person raising a family in the New York/ Pennsylvania area. She wrote the following viewpoint for the blog Words from Poor Folks *to help readers better understand the plight of impoverished families in America.*

Being poor exacts a heavy toll, not just economically like people might expect, but also physically, emotionally, and even socially. Living in poverty means stretching money and food thin and often doing without, but it also means living in a constant state of exhaustion, hopelessness, and fear that no matter how hard one works to get ahead, it won't be enough. Poverty wears down a person's spirit, compromises physical and mental health, undermines self-confidence, and strains relationships. It promotes social isolation, shame, anger, and jealousy. Hard-working families should be able to make ends meet in America without the debasing experience of poverty.

Today, I did something I never thought I'd do. I yelled at my son for being hungry. Oh sure, there are many parents nodding in agreement because they've done the same thing. Many have yelled at their kids for asking for one more snack right before dinner was served or for wanting to eat junk food out of boredom. That's not why I yelled. I yelled because I didn't have extra food to give him and I was taking my frustration out on him. He wasn't doing anything wrong. He's just a kid, a 7 year old who is full of energy and constantly growing. Of course he's hungry often. That's what kids do. However, I didn't have enough food for anyone to have extras. Everything has to be rationed out over a week or more. Food stuff needs to be stretched. Already angry and frustrated with our situation, I lost my cool when my child asked a simple question—because I knew there was nothing I could do to change it in that moment. My anger turned to worry, another constant feeling in my daily life, as I wondered if this would create food issues in my child. Will he be afraid to eat, knowing that we might not have enough the next day?

I'm 35 years old. I am a mother and a wife. I am college educated, degreed, and I have held a professional license. I have been working since the age of 18. Until now. I live in poverty. I am poor. My family is poor.

Living in poverty is like being punched in the face over and over and over on a daily basis. It's pulling yourself out of a hole, only to fall over a cliff.

What It Means to Be Poor

When I say I am poor, I don't mean that it's going to take me two weeks to save for a new iPad or the next iWhatever. I don't mean that I'll need a coupon to shop at J.Crew. I mean that I have saved my kids Halloween candy for times when my blood sugar gets too low after a day of not eating because I can't afford enough food for 3 square meals for the entire family. It means that having my heat set above 60 degrees is a luxury. It means that the needle on my gas gauge is constantly hovering at E. It means that we wear our clothes several times before laundering because we can't afford the fees to use the washing machines. It means the thrift shop is damn expensive. It means so many more things that we don't often think about unless we're living in poverty. As a culture, we are disconnected to the idea of not having access to the most basic needs. Consumerism and materialism are supposedly signs of a healthy economy and successful nation, environment be damned, and a blind eye towards those less advantaged is a requirement.

A No-Frills Life

Our story of poverty doesn't come with credit card bills, expensive cable packages, luxury toys. It's not that anyone should be judged for why they are poor, but people naturally ask, mostly out of curiosity and sometimes to find information to justify their lack of care for your position, for a way to blame you for your own situation. It makes it easier to detach. We have both been hard workers for over a decade. We have played by the rules. It still got us. I am currently unemployed—and that's not for a lack of effort. My husband lost a fairly good job over a year ago and we've been pulled down a spiral ever since. His period of unemployment meant we burned through our savings and our emergency fund. While I am still unemployed (to be fair, I do walk dogs or babysit on occasion for some cash, but those times are few and far between), my husband is currently working three jobs. Three jobs. My husband is not college educated. He has worked on the warehouse/shipping/receiving side of retail for a very long time and is good at what he does. He's very strong, enjoys physical labor, and is a hard worker. His three jobs are retail-based. Two of them pay exactly minimum wage. The third pays just above that. He is constantly applying for jobs on a weekly basis, as am I. With three jobs, you can imagine he works many hours. There have been weeks were he worked all three jobs back to back with maybe an hour or two in between. Thanksgiving to the New Year were brutal. He would often work nearly 30 hours in a row, come home to sleep for a few hours, then go back for another cycle of 30 hours. It's been brutal on his health and our family.

Anger and Inequity

Will someone stop for a moment and tell me in what world is it considered moral for a person to work three jobs and still be unable to support their family. It just isn't right. Living in poverty is like being punched in the face over and over and over on a daily basis. It's pulling yourself out of a hole, only to fall over a cliff. Every step in the right direction is rewarded with a hearty push several steps back. The changes to one's mental health when living in poverty can be astonishing. I suffered a miscarriage years ago and I knew anger and sadness then. I made my way through it and survived. I didn't think I would feel such strong emotions again. I was wrong. The anger is back. Anger is for everything. I'm angry I am in this situation. I am angry I'm not good enough for proper employment. I'm angry my children are living through this. I am angry at my husband. I'm angry at Christians who preach against me, ignoring the words of Christ. I'm angry at politicians who vote against people like me. I'm angry at a society that views me as a leech, as a welfare queen, as someone who deserves to be on the bottom of humanity's shoe.

The hunger is extraordinary. There is a constant gnawing in your stomach, an empty feeling that has taken up permanent residence.

Envy for Material Goods

There is jealousy. I've never been a materialistic person and neither has my husband. We have never felt the need to keep up with the Joneses—no desire for brand name clothing, big screen TVs, or the latest electronic gadget. We've never had cable. I liked to shop when I genuinely needed things, but I wouldn't overspend or buy things I couldn't afford. I never owned a credit card. Fashion magazines were fun and I'd laugh at the implication that a woman should spend $200.00 on a pair of jeans. Now, I'm jealous at anyone who can afford to buy $15.00 jeans on sale at Old Navy. Friends post their "OMG! Kohl's haul!" on Facebook, posting pictures of their new boots, sweaters, jeans, yoga pants, etc. Where I would once say, "oh, those boots are cute," I am now filled with plain old bitter envy. I wish I could just look at my boots, the ones with the rip in them, decide it was time to buy new ones, and walk out the door to buy a new pair. I wish I could say, "Gee, I sure am sick of wearing the same two shirts day in and day out," and go to a store a buy a few new shirts that actually fit. I can't. I have clothes that are finally showing their age and their wear. Threads are falling lose, seams opening, little holes throughout fabric, buttons are disappearing. An acquaintance said to me recently, "You actually look like a poor person." Gee, thanks. I didn't know there is a certain look for poor people. . . . My husband spent a few months with holes in his work pants. I sewed them up as best I could, but eventually the fabric would be worn down so much that there wasn't much to sew. He took to wearing black shorts under his pants (also black) so the holes wouldn't be as noticeable. Thankfully, he received a couple of new pairs for Christmas. He also spent months walking with holes in his shoes. His sneakers literally fell off his feet one day and he was left with boots that were no longer waterproof and had a hole or two. He'd walk to and from work in rain and snow in those boots. Forget socks. He doesn't own a pair without holes. We were blessed by a couple of friends who chipped in to buy him a new pair of sturdy, waterproof work boots.

It's hard for others to deal with the overwhelming depression and hopelessness that accompanies poverty.

A Limited Social Life

Jealousy isn't limited to clothing. I've been jealous that friends can do wild and crazy things like buy a full tank of gas, get new brakes for their cars, buy a pack of toilet paper, eat. Food is a big one. In this age of social media, one can guarantee that at least 3 ultra-filtered Instagram photos of a friend's lunch will scroll on by on their computer screen each day. Back in the day, I would just note that so-and-so had a bagel for lunch and I'd go on with my day. Now, I just sit there and wish it was me. I wish I had a plate full of good food to obnoxiously photograph, but I don't. It's the food that really drove the issue home for me not too long ago. I had taken my children to Ikea. We weren't there to buy anything. It was damn cold, we were tired of being cooped up in the house, and there weren't many options for a free place to play. Ikea has a play zone for my older child. My daughter is more than happy to walk around the store, sitting on sofas and chairs. I love Ikea because it's fun to imagine having different furniture and organization. While there, I bought my kids lunch. They had one of their specials going and kiddie meals were free! My kids each had a meal, which included drinks. I didn't get anything for me. As they ate, I would pick at their plates, stealing a bite here and there. I looked at everyone eating around me and that's when the tears, which I fought very hard to hold back, started to flow. I wanted so badly to be able to order something for myself. I was starving and the little bites of steamed veggies and mac 'n' cheese weren't very filling. I hadn't eaten yet that day and found myself just staring at the plates of strangers, wishing I was free to get myself something to eat. I found myself glaring at people through my tears as they took plates and bowls half full of food to the trash center—what a waste of food! Never before had I been tempted to say, "hey, I'll take that," than I was on that day. My son noticed me wiping tears and asked what was wrong. I lied and told him I took a bite of his sister's squash and it must have had some sort of spice on it and I was reacting to that. He believed me for a moment, taking a last bite of his mashed potatoes before pushing the plate over to me and telling me he was full. More tears to fight off.

Extraordinary Hunger

That brings me to the hunger. The hunger is extraordinary. There is a constant gnawing in your stomach, an empty feeling that has taken up permanent residence. Even as you're eating a meal, you feel the hunger. It never goes away because you don't know when you're going to eat again. You don't know if your next meal will be something proper or if it'll be half a fun-sized bag of M&M's that you hoarded from your kids' Halloween haul or nothing at all. It's an ever-present gastric uncertainty. As food stamp benefits continue to be cut and food pantries struggle to feed communities, that uncertainty will just continue. I hate to think of my children feeling the same way. They get first dibs on all food that comes through this house. There are many days when my kids get their three meals and I get half of one and my husband . . . well, I never see him because he is working all the time, but he barely eats, too. This is obviously unhealthy. Our health has tanked over the last year. I've been told I constantly look tired. My eyes are more sunken, devoid of light. My skin is dry, blemished, and overall just blah. My hair is brittle and I lose a lot of it on a daily basis. I'm constantly weak. My husband is a very strong man, but he has lost an alarming amount of muscle and strength in the past year. The two of us are constantly exhausted. Part of that is the hunger, part of it is emotional.

A Spiral of Despair

The emotions certainly take their toll. Hopelessness is unbearable. I was once someone that my friends would always look to for a positive thought and encouraging words. I always managed to see the good in every situation. I try my best to hold onto that, but it's been slipping away quickly. Fear is constant. You're always afraid of what's next. I'm afraid of opening my bills to find new late fees. I'm afraid of losing utilities. I'm afraid of being evicted because we can't afford our rent. You want to think positive, but the idea of "what's next" is always looming. Things that might seem minor to one person can spell disaster for a family in poverty. Last week, my husband told me my tail light was out. This is typically not a big deal for many people. To us, it's terrifying. We don t have the money for a new tail light. But, it's illegal here to have one out. Our cops here are very good at pulling you over for broken lights, outdated stickers, etc. Obviously, it's the law to keep your car in check. We know this. I've always been great at keeping my car well-maintained. My inspections were always done on time, lights would be replaced immediately, oil is always changed, I never drove on gas fumes at the needle hovered on E. It's all different now. Small things are big things. Monumental things. The idea of needing a tail light, an inspection, or a new tire due to the 100's of pot holes created by tons of snow this Winter is enough to send me into a panic. Weather is terrorizing these days. Two of my husband's jobs can be called off due to snow or ice because the trucks can't get to them, so they tell staff to stay home. We've had storm after storm after storm this season. My husband has missed so much work, not by choice, due to snow and ice. We added it up and discovered that he missed enough to pay for nearly two months of rent. Same for me—no doggies to walk in this weather because people are staying home.

The future is more than uncertain and it feels that the ground under me can open at any moment and swallow me whole.

Poverty Strains Friendships

Poverty is isolating. Friends eventually fade away because they think you're ignoring them when you constantly turn down their invites to dinner or events. They take it personal no matter how many times you insist it's not. Your children's social lives suffer for the same reason—you can't afford to send them to many birthday parties or playdates. Trips to zoos, museums, and other fun places with admission fees are extremely limited. People eventually tire of you being unavailable to come out for fun and they stop calling and texting. And maybe I should say those people aren't friends in the first place, but it doesn't take the pain away. It doesn't make me hurt less for my children. Conversely, you have friends who know you're in poverty and they try to brainstorm, try to help you through it. You say thank you a million times, but it's not enough. After a while, trying to save you is boring and when they realize they didn't fix you, they get annoyed. I've been called everything by people who were supposed to be my friends. Because I can't snap my fingers and make things work perfectly and because that fact depresses the f--- out of me, I've been called useless, manipulative, worthless, unmotivated. No one wants to hear that you have tried all the options that they suggested and they didn't work out. No one wants to hear that you know exactly why a suggestion won't work. They don't understand why you can't "just move" or "just declare bankruptcy" or just swing around a pole (note: no one ever suggests that my husband sell his body for cash . . . but quite a few people have presented it as an option for me). This isn't to say they are not well-meaning—and they certainly are not under appreciated by me—but they eventually get exasperated when you explain time and time again why certain suggestions don't work. They want to fix you, fix you now, get you to shut the f--- up about being poor. It's hard for others to deal with the overwhelming depression and hopelessness that accompanies poverty. It's hard for them to hear that you don't want to get up in the morning anymore, that you just want to end it all. So, it's sometimes easier to be angry at the poor person, to convince yourself that they just don't want to work for it, and keep your distance from them. Many friendships have been strained by poverty.

Second-Guessing One's Self Is Common

However, no one can be as hard on you as you are on yourself. I spend hours per day telling myself how much I suck. If only I had done this or done that. I know our circumstances were beyond our control. I know how hard we try every single day. But, it doesn't stop me from doubting myself, from putting myself down. It doesn't stop the shame. I feel like a leech. I'm told by my friendly clergymen, my wonderful politicians, and by people I know and once called friends that I am a burden on society. I'm a taker. If only I worked harder. If only I wanted to stop being poor and getting handouts, then everything would turn around and I would be rich. If only I would pray harder, attend the correct church, and read an ancient book that I have read cover to cover many times in the past. Then God would just bestow His blessings upon me. Or, I should really just consider putting some positive energy out into the Universe. If I meditate and tell the Universe that I want money, money will come and everything will be fixed. The constant shouts from society's peanut gallery telling me how the poor are worthless and damned help shape my inner dialogue and I begin to agree with them. I am worthless. I deserve the shame I feel.

Still in Need

It's hard to accept help when your inner dialogue tells you that you are useless. People tell me to be willing to accept help, I'll be able to pay it forward someday. Without friends and the kindness of strangers, we wouldn't have had a Christmas for our kids. My car payment would not have been paid for a couple of months, my husband would still have holes in his boots, and my car would still be uninspected and I'd be in deep shit. And we're still here, still in need.

I sit here now, writing this at my desk that is piled with overdue utility bills and a statement from my landlord telling us they are pursuing legal action against us because our rent is currently 17 days late. I have multiple windows open on my computer—several for job applications for me, several job applications for my husband to look at once he's home from work, a few for charity searches, another for prayer requests, and another for a site that offers emotional support and solidarity for people like me. The future is more than uncertain and it feels that the ground under me can open at any moment and swallow me whole.

And so I do pray. I do hope. I work hard to get our family out of this hell hole and so does my husband. I am grateful in ways that I cannot fully express for all the help that has come to my family in recent months from both friends and strangers. It reminds us that even though life is pure shit right now, there are bright spots. The good exists. So, we continue to focus on that. I hope to eventually write about how we struggled, survived, and came out on top. Until then, be nice to the poor folk. You can have all the assumptions in the world about how they got there, how they feel, how much they "take," but you can never really know their true story—humans deserve compassion.

7

Poverty in America
Is Greatly Exaggerated

Robert Rector and Rachel Sheffield

Robert Rector is a senior research fellow in the domestic policy studies department at the Heritage Foundation, a conservative think tank. Rachel Sheffield is a policy analyst in the DeVos Center for Religion and Civil Society at Heritage.

Claims that more than thirty million Americans live in poverty are wildly exaggerated. In reality, the typical poor family in the United States has enough nutritious food to eat, a safe home to live in, and decent clothing to wear. What's more, they are overwhelming likely to also have such modern amenities as a car, air conditioner, refrigerator, microwave, cable television, clothes washer and dryer, cell phones, and even video gaming systems. America's poor rarely report going hungry, receive sufficient medical care, and generally have enough money to meet their basic needs, such as utilities. The "poor" in America do not suffer real deprivation and would not be considered impoverished elsewhere in the world.

Each year for the past two decades, the U.S. Census Bureau has reported that over 30 million Americans were living in "poverty." In recent years, the Census has reported that one in seven Americans are poor. But what does it mean to be "poor" in America? How poor are America's poor?

For most Americans, the word "poverty" suggests destitution: an inability to provide a family with nutritious food, clothing, and reasonable shelter. For example, the Poverty Pulse poll taken by the Catholic Campaign for Human Development asked the general public: "How would you describe being poor in the U.S.?" The overwhelming majority of responses focused on homelessness, hunger or not being able to eat properly, and not being able to meet basic needs. That perception is bolstered by news stories about poverty that routinely feature homelessness and hunger.

Poor families certainly struggle to make ends meet, but in most cases, they are struggling to pay for air conditioning and the cable TV bill as well as to put food on the table.

Yet if poverty means lacking nutritious food, adequate warm housing, and clothing for a family, relatively few of the more than 30 million people identified as being "in poverty" by the Census Bureau could be characterized as poor. While material hardship definitely exists in the United States, it is restricted in scope and severity. The average poor person, as defined by the government, has a living standard far higher than the public imagines.

As scholar James Q. Wilson has stated, "The poorest Americans today live a better life than all but the richest persons a hundred years ago." In 2005, the typical household defined as poor by the government had a car and air conditioning. For entertainment, the household had two color televisions, cable or satellite TV, a DVD player, and a VCR. If there were children, especially boys, in the home, the family had a game system, such as an Xbox or a PlayStation. In the kitchen, the household had a refrigerator, an oven and stove, and a microwave. Other household conveniences included a clothes washer, clothes dryer, ceiling fans, a cordless phone, and a coffee maker.

A Typical Family

The home of the typical poor family was not overcrowded and was in good repair. In fact, the typical poor American had more living space than the average European. The typical poor American family was also able to obtain medical care when needed. By its own report, the typical family was not hungry and had sufficient funds during the past year to meet all essential needs.

Poor families certainly struggle to make ends meet, but in most cases, they are struggling to pay for air conditioning and the cable TV bill as well as to put food on the table. Their living standards are far different from the images of dire deprivation promoted by activists and the mainstream media.

Regrettably, annual Census reports not only exaggerate current poverty, but also suggest that the number of poor persons and their living conditions have remained virtually unchanged for four decades or more. In reality, the living conditions of poor Americans have shown significant improvement over time.

> *Accurate information about the extent and severity of social problems is imperative for the development of effective public policy.*

Consumer items that were luxuries or significant purchases for the middle class a few decades ago have become commonplace in poor households. In part, this is caused by a normal downward trend in price following the introduction of a new product. Initially, new products tend to be expensive and available only to the affluent. Over time, prices fall sharply, and the product saturates the entire population, including poor households.

As a rule of thumb, poor households tend to obtain modern conveniences about a dozen years after the middle class.

Today, most poor families have conveniences that were unaffordable to the middle class not too long ago.

A Range of Living Conditions

However, there is a range of living conditions within the poverty population. The average poor family does not represent every poor family. Although most poor families are well housed, a small minority are homeless.

Fortunately, the number of homeless Americans has not increased during the current recession. Although most poor families are well fed and have a fairly stable food supply, a sizeable minority experiences temporary restraints in food supply at various times during the year. The number of families experiencing such temporary food shortages has increased somewhat during the current economic downturn.

Of course, to the families experiencing these problems, their comparative infrequency is irrelevant. To a family that has lost its home and is living in a homeless shelter, the fact that only 0.5 percent of families shared this experience in 2009 is no comfort. The distress and fear for the future that the family experiences are real and devastating. Public policy must deal with that distress. However, accurate information about the extent and severity of social problems is imperative for the development of effective public policy.

In discussions about poverty, however, misunderstanding and exaggeration are commonplace. Over the long term, exaggeration has the potential to promote a substantial misallocation of limited resources for a government that is facing massive future deficits. In addition, exaggeration and misinformation obscure the nature, extent, and causes of real material deprivation, thereby hampering the development of well-targeted, effective programs to reduce the problem. Poverty is an issue of serious social concern, and accurate information about that problem is always essential in crafting public policy.

Living Conditions of the Poor

Each year, the U.S. Census Bureau releases its annual report on income and poverty. This report, though widely publicized by the press, provides only a bare count of the number of Americans who are allegedly poor. It provides no data on or description of their actual living conditions.

[The Residential Energy Consumption Survey] showed that median poor households most frequently had the following 14 items: air conditioning, a clothes washer, a clothes dryer, ceiling fans, and a cordless phone.

This does not mean that such information is not available. The federal government conducts several other surveys that provide detailed information on the living conditions of the poor. These surveys provide a very different sense of American poverty. They reveal that the actual standard of living among America's poor is far higher than the public imagines and that, in fact, most of the persons whom the government defines as "in poverty" are not poor in any ordinary sense of the term. Regrettably, these detailed surveys are almost never reported in the mainstream press.

One of the most interesting surveys that measures actual living conditions is the Residential Energy Consumption Survey (RECS), which the Department of Energy has conducted regularly since 1980. The RECS survey measures energy consumption and ownership of various conveniences by U.S. households. It also provides information on households at different income levels, including poor households. . . .

The analysis showed that median poor households most frequently had the following 14 items: air conditioning, a clothes washer, a clothes dryer, ceiling fans, and a cordless phone.

For entertainment, these households had two color televisions, cable or satellite TV, a DVD player, and a VCR.

In the kitchen, these poor households had a refrigerator, an oven and stove, a microwave, and a coffee maker.

These items may then be considered representative of the living standards of the median or typical poor U.S. household in 2005.

The median poor household had five fewer amenities than the median household in the general population. Specifically, the typical poor household lacked the following items that were in the typical middle-income household: a personal computer, Internet access, a computer printer, a dishwasher, and a cell phone.

Only 2 percent of poor domiciles have "severe" physical problems, the most common of which is sharing a bathroom with another household living in the building.

Amenities in Poor Families with Children

Poor families with children have more conveniences and amenities than other poor families. In 2005, the median amenity score for poor families with children was 16. We examined all poor families with children with an amenity score of 16 to determine which items appeared most frequently in these homes.

- These homes typically had both air conditioning and a personal computer.

- For entertainment, they typically had cable or satellite TV, three color televisions, a DVD player, a VCR, and a video game system, such as an Xbox or Play Station.

- In the kitchen, they had a refrigerator, a stove and oven, a microwave, and an automatic coffee maker.

- Other amenities included a cell phone, a cordless phone, and a clothes washer.

These conveniences may be considered representative of the living standards of the median or typical poor family with children in 2005.

Housing and Poverty

Of course, the typical poor family could have a host of modern conveniences and still live in dilapidated, overcrowded housing. However, data from other government surveys show that this is not the case. Poor Americans are well housed and rarely overcrowded. In fact, the houses and apartments of America's poor are quite spacious by international standards. The typical poor American has considerably more living space than does the average European.

Forty-three percent of all poor households own their own homes. The average home owned by persons classified as poor by the Census Bureau is a three-bedroom house with one-and-a-half baths, a garage, and a porch or patio.

Nearly all of the houses and apartments of the poor are in good condition. According to the government's data, only one in 10 has moderate physical problems. Only 2 percent of poor domiciles have "severe" physical problems, the most common of which is sharing a bathroom with another household living in the building.

Food Shortages, Nutrition, and Poverty

It is possible that most poor households could be well housed and have many modern conveniences but still face chronic food shortages and under-nutrition. Poor families might have microwaves but a limited and sporadic supply of food to put in the microwave. Government surveys show that this is not the case for the overwhelming majority of poor families.

On average, the poor are well nourished. The average consumption of protein, vitamins, and minerals is virtually the same for poor and middle-class children. In most cases, it is well above recommended norms. Poor children actually consume more meat than higher-income children consume, and their protein intake averages 100 percent above recommended levels. In fact, most poor children are super-nourished and grow up to be, on average, one inch taller and 10 pounds heavier than the GIs who stormed the beaches of Normandy in World War II.

However, even though the poor, in general, have an ample food supply, some do suffer from temporary food shortages. For example, a poor household with an adequate long-term food supply might need temporarily to cut back meals, eat cheap food, or go without if cash and food stamps run out at the end of the month.

Still, government data show that most poor households do not suffer even from temporary food shortages. Ninety-two percent of poor households assert that they always had "enough food to eat" during the previous four months, although 26 percent of these did not always have the foods that they would have preferred. Some 6 percent of poor households state that they "sometimes" did not have enough food, and 1.5 percent say they "often" did not have enough food.

The bottom line is that, although a small portion of poor households report temporary food shortages, the overwhelming majority of poor households report that they consistently have enough food to eat.

At any point in 2009, roughly one person out of 1,250 in the general population or one out of 180 poor persons was homeless in the literal sense of being on the street and without shelter.

Temporary food shortages have increased during the current recession but still remain atypical among poor households. During 2009, less than one poor household in five experienced even a single instance of "reduced food intake and disrupted eating patterns" due to a lack of financial resources.

Strikingly, only 4 percent of poor children experienced even a single instance of "reduced food intake and disrupted eating patterns" due to a lack of financial resources. . . .

Poverty and Homelessness

The mainstream press and activist groups also frequently conflate poverty with homelessness. News stories about poverty often feature homeless families living "on the street." This depiction is seriously misleading because only a small portion of persons "living in poverty" will become homeless over the course of a year. The overwhelming majority of the poor reside throughout the year in non-crowded housing that is in good repair.

The 2009 *Annual Homeless Assessment Report* published by the U.S. Department of Housing and Urban Development (HUD) states that on a given night in 2009, some 643,000 persons in the U.S. were homeless (without permanent domicile). This means that at any given time, one out of 470 persons in the general population or one out of 70 persons with incomes below the poverty level was homeless.

Moreover, two-thirds of these 643,000 homeless persons were residing in emergency shelters or transitional housing. Only 240,000 were without shelter. These "unsheltered" individuals were "on the street," meaning that they were living in cars, abandoned buildings, alleyways, or parks. At any point in 2009, roughly one person out of 1,250 in the general population or one out of 180 poor persons was homeless in the literal sense of being on the street and without shelter.

Homelessness is usually a transitional condition. Individuals typically lose housing, reside in an emergency shelter for a few weeks or months, and then reenter permanent housing. The transitional nature of homelessness means that many more people become temporarily homeless over the course of a year than are homeless at any single point in time. . . .

Despite news stories that assert that the current recession has caused a great increase in homelessness, homeless shelter use, in general, has not increased during the current economic downturn. In addition, shelters are not overcrowded. On a typical night, shelters have an average vacancy rate of 10 percent.

While the overall number of homeless has not increased during the current recession, there has been a small increase in the number of families with children who use homeless shelters. Some 168,000 families with children resided in a homeless shelter for at least one night during all of 2010. This figure was up from 130,000 in 2007. The increase of 38,000 families represents only one family out every 1,000 families with children. While the misfortune is real for the families involved, these numbers scarcely show a tidal wave of increased homelessness.

Only 13 percent of poor households report that a family member needed to go to a doctor or hospital at some point in the prior year but was unable because the family could not afford the cost.

Although news stories often suggest that poverty and homelessness are similar, this is inaccurate. In reality, the gap between the living conditions of a homeless person and the typical poor household is proportionately as great as the gap between the poor household and a middle-class family in the suburbs.

Essential Needs

Although the public equates poverty with physical deprivation, the overwhelming majority of poor households do not experience any form of physical deprivation. Some 70 percent of poor households report that during the course of the past year, they were able to meet "all essential expenses," including mortgage, rent, utility bills, and important medical care.

It is widely supposed that the poor are unable to obtain medical care, but in reality, only 13 percent of poor households report that a family member needed to go to a doctor or hospital at some point in the prior year but was unable because the family could not afford the cost.

Public Understanding of Poverty

In 2005, the typical poor household, as defined by the government, had air conditioning and a car. For entertainment, the household had two color televisions, cable or satellite TV, a DVD player, and a VCR. In the kitchen, it had a refrigerator, an oven and stove, and a microwave. Other household conveniences included a clothes washer, clothes dryer, ceiling fans, a cordless phone, and a coffee maker. The family was able to obtain medical care when needed. Their home was not overcrowded and was in good repair. By its own report, the family was not hungry and had sufficient funds during the past year to meet all essential needs.

The overwhelming majority of the public do not regard a family living in these conditions as poor. For example, a poll conducted in June 2009 asked a nationally representative sample of the public whether they agreed or disagreed with the following statement: "A family in the U.S. that has a decent, un-crowded house or apartment to live in, ample food to eat, access to medical care, a car, cable television, air conditioning and a microwave at home should not be considered poor."

A full 80 percent of Republicans and 77 percent of Democrats agreed that a family living in those living conditions should not be considered poor. . . .

Misrepresenting Poverty in America

As noted, for the average American, the word "poverty" implies significant material hardship and deprivation. Politicians, activists, and the mainstream media reinforce this image, asserting that each year, over 35 million Americans live in chronic material deprivation, unable to obtain "the basic material necessities of life." . . .

At any given time, only a small portion of the more than 35 million "poor" Americans will experience the sort of dramatic deprivation presented in the [media].

Protestations by anti-poverty activists almost always involve two incompatible ideas: that poverty in America is widespread, affecting as many as one in seven Americans, and that being poor in this country means serious material deprivation. The fusion of these two notions leads to a profound misrepresentation of the actual living conditions in the nation. . . .

The interlocking assertions that poverty is widespread, affecting one in seven Americans, and that the poor live in desperate conditions are both ideologically necessary for the Left. Together, they provide justification for policies to greatly expand the welfare state and further "spread the wealth." But if one or both assertions proves to be untrue, the impetus for expanding the welfare state is greatly undermined. . . .

While substantial hardship does occur in U.S. society, it is limited in scope. At any given time, only a small portion of the more than 35 million "poor" Americans will experience the sort of dramatic deprivation presented in the above newscasts. Moreover, when dramatic hardship does occur, it is generally temporary or caused by multiple behavioral problems in the home.

Ironically, suggesting that tens of millions of poor Americans suffer from chronic substantial deprivation actually makes solving social problems more difficult. Such misrepresentation leads to a misallocation of resources and, by obscuring the causes of deprivation, impedes the development of effective countermeasures. . . .

What Is Poverty?

In 2010, the U.S. Census Bureau declared that one in seven Americans lived "in poverty." Catholic Charities has declared, "The existence of such widespread poverty amidst such enormous wealth is a moral and social wound in the soul of the country."

To the average American, the word "poverty" implies significant material deprivation, an inability to provide a family with adequate nutritious food, reasonable shelter, and clothing. Activists reinforce this view, declaring that being poor in the U.S. means being "unable to obtain the basic material necessities of life." The news media amplify this idea: Most news stories on poverty feature homeless families, people living in crumbling shacks, or lines of the downtrodden eating in soup kitchens.

The actual living conditions of America's poor are far different from these images. In 2005, the typical household defined as poor by the government had a car and air conditioning. For entertainment, the household had two color televisions, cable or satellite TV, a DVD player, and a VCR. If there were children, especially boys, in the home, the family had a game system, such as an Xbox or PlayStation. In the kitchen, the household had a refrigerator, an oven and stove, and a microwave. Other household conveniences included a clothes washer, a clothes dryer, ceiling fans, a cordless phone, and a coffee maker.

The home of the typical poor family was not overcrowded and was in good repair. The family was able to obtain medical care when needed. By its own report, the family was not hungry and had sufficient funds during the past year to meet all essential needs.

Poor families clearly struggle to make ends meet, but in most cases, they are struggling to pay for air conditioning and cable TV while putting food on the table. The current recession has increased the number of Americans who are poor, but it does not appear to have greatly reduced the living standards of the average poor family.

Foundations of Public Policy

True, the average poor family does not represent every poor family. There is a range of living conditions among the poor. Some poor households fare better than the average household described above. Others are worse off. Although the overwhelming majority of the poor are well housed, at any single point in time during the recession in 2009, around one in 70 poor persons was homeless. Although the majority of poor families have an adequate and reasonably steady supply of food, many worry about keeping food on the table, and one in five experienced temporary food shortages at various times in 2009.

Those who are without food or homeless will find no comfort in the fact that their condition is relatively infrequent. Their distress is real and a serious concern.

Nonetheless, wise public policy cannot be based on misinformation or misunderstanding. Anti-poverty policy must be based on an accurate assessment of actual living conditions and the causes of deprivation. In the long term, grossly exaggerating the extent and severity of material deprivation in the U.S. will benefit neither the poor, the economy, nor society as a whole.

8

US Poverty Rate Reduced Thanks to Safety-Net Programs

Zachary A. Goldfarb

Zachary A. Goldfarb is a Washington Post *staff writer who focuses on President Barack Obama's economic, financial, and fiscal policies.*

In the fifty years since President Lyndon Johnson launched the war on poverty, government safety-net programs, such as food stamps and unemployment insurance, have helped reduce poverty in America by 10 percent, according to a new study. More recently, and of particular note, the US poverty rate did not soar during the 2007–2009 economic recession, evidence, analysts say, that President Barack Obama's broad expansion of safety-net programs and tax credits during the economic crisis worked to protect the country's most vulnerable residents. Such a clear record of success is evidence that America's safety-net programs must be protected into the future.

Government programs such as food stamps and unemployment insurance have made significant progress in easing the plight of the poor in the half-century since the launch of the war on poverty, according to a major new study.

But the nation's economy has made far less progress lifting people out of poverty without the need for government services.

The findings by a group of academic researchers at Columbia University paint a mixed picture of the United States nearly 50 years after [President] Lyndon B. Johnson announced in his January 1964 State of the Union address that he would wage a war on poverty. They also contradict the official poverty rate, which suggests there has been no decline in the percentage of Americans experiencing poverty since then.

According to the new research, the safety net helped reduce the percentage of Americans in poverty from 26 percent in 1967 to 16 percent in 2012. The results were especially striking during the most recent economic downturn, when the poverty rate barely budged despite a massive increase in unemployment.

The research suggests that Congress must preserve the safety net as a critical tool to help the poor.

While the government has helped keep poverty at bay, the economy by itself has failed to improve the lives of the very poor over the past 50 years. Without taking into account the role of government policy, more Americans—29 percent— would be in poverty today, compared with 27 percent in 1967.

The Safety-Net Debate

The research has already resonated in Washington, where there are sharp debates in Congress about whether to trim the safety net.

For the White House, where President [Barack] Obama and top advisers have been briefed on the study, the research suggests that Congress must preserve the safety net as a critical tool to help the poor—at the same time that additional steps are taken to make sure that lower-income Americans earn high-enough wages to escape poverty.

"It gives you a deep appreciation for what public programs do today and how much more they do today than in the past," said Jason Furman, chairman of Obama's Council of Economic Advisers. "But it also gives you a sense of how little progress we've made on incomes and raising incomes in the past several decades and the importance of doing that going forward in order to continue to make progress on poverty."

Other analysts note that the dramatic expansion of the safety net comes with unintended consequences, including increased dependency for the poor.

Scott Winship, a fellow at the conservative Manhattan Institute, said the safety net plays an important and helpful role "during downturns, but then when the economy turns around, the expanded safety net has acted as a poverty trap, in essence lulling people and preventing them from pursuing work."

About the Study

The study was led by Christopher Wimer and Liana Fox, researchers at the Columbia Population Research Center, and joined by professors Irwin Garfinkel, Neeraj Kaushal and Jane Waldfogel. They made use of a change in how the U.S. government began measuring poverty in 2010.

Until then, the U.S. Census evaluated poverty based only on a limited measure of the income and expenses of Americans. From 1967 through 2012, the official measure showed poverty increasing from 14 percent of the population to 15 percent, often falling during periods of economic strength and rising during weakness.

But starting three years ago, the government began publishing an alternative measure that took into account the full range of expenses the poor face and the government benefits they receive. The Columbia researchers went further, using

that standard and tracing it back in time to evaluate the evo-
lution of poverty since the Johnson era.

---

*One of the most striking findings for the researchers was
how poverty stayed stable during the financial crisis and
Great Recession thanks to a dramatic expansion of the
safety net.*

Among the researchers' discoveries was that deep poverty—incomes below 50 percent of the poverty line—has been
stable at 5 percent of the population for about 40 years and
that the safety net has grown especially powerful in protecting
children from poverty.

"That means the safety net is working effectively for the
most vulnerable families and kids," Waldfogel said.

One of the most striking findings for the researchers was
how poverty stayed stable during the financial crisis and Great
Recession thanks to a dramatic expansion of the safety net, including enhanced unemployment benefits, more-generous
food stamps and tax credits for the poor.

Weathering the Recession

In previous and shallower recessions, poverty increased more
than it did during the 2007-to-2009 downturn. For example,
as the economy slowed and fell into recession in 1990, the
poverty rate, including the impact of the safety net, rose 1.5
percentage points to 20.7 percent.

By contrast, in the far worse recent recession, with a much
higher level of unemployment, the poverty rate rose only 0.8
percentage points.

"It's sort of remarkable," Wimer said. Without the safety
net, "poverty would have risen by five or six percentage points
from 2007 through 2012."

More recently, in the slow-going economic recovery, this
alternative poverty rate has climbed a bit more, to 16 per-

cent—a reflection, researchers say, of the fact that Americans are losing benefits as they return to work, a positive outcome that still involves costs such as transportation.

Armed with this type of evidence, White House officials say they will work aggressively to try to protect existing safety-net programs at the same time they seek to lift the wages of people in need, for example by fighting for an increase in the minimum wage.

"We have to defend nutritional assistance and unemployment insurance that made that progress on reducing poverty possible, but we also have to address the reasons that poverty hasn't improved in market incomes," Furman said. "When you cut the wages for low-income people, adjusted for inflation, you're not going to make as much progress on reducing poverty for low-income Americans."

9

The United States Lags on Poverty Compared to Other Nations

Elise Gould and Hilary Wething

Elise Gould is director of health policy research at the Economic Policy Institute (EPI), a nonprofit liberal think tank that advocates for low-to-moderate-income families. Hilary Wething is a senior research assistant at EPI.

According to research published in the 2014 edition of The State of Working America *by the Economic Policy Institute, the poverty rate in the United States is markedly higher than other countries that are part of the Organisation for Economic Co-operation and Development (OECD), a global consortium of thirty-four countries founded in the 1960s to stimulate world trade and economic progress. The report found that the extent of child poverty in the United States is particularly severe—almost five times higher than that of Iceland, which had the lowest rate. Among OECD countries, the United States has the dubious distinction of having the highest poverty rate and one of the lowest rates of social expenditures for the poor.*

Poverty rates in the United States increased over the 2000s, a trend exacerbated by the Great Recession and its aftermath. By 2010, just over 46 million people fell below the U.S. Census Bureau's official poverty line (according to data from the Current Population Survey). This preview of *The State of Working America, 12th Edition* puts the U.S. experience with poverty in an international context, comparing the lower end of the wage and income distribution in the United States with that of "peer" countries, largely countries within the Organisation for Economic Co-operation and Development (OECD) with roughly similar GDP [gross domestic product] per hour worked as the United States.

The first part of this preview provides a general comparison of poverty and the earnings distribution in the United States and peer countries. Next, it examines the extent to which resources go to the bottom, focusing specifically on the tax and transfer system that redistributes market income and provides a safety net to keep people out of poverty, or to help those who fall into poverty due to unexpected job losses or other reversals get back on their feet.

Inequality in the United States is so severe that low-earning U.S. workers are actually worse off than low-earning workers in all but seven peer countries.

Poverty and the Earnings Distribution

One particular point of interest in international comparisons is the ratio of earnings (wages) at the 10th percentile of the earnings distribution to earnings of the median worker. This measures how workers at the bottom fare in relation to the typical worker, with a lower number implying more inequality. Earnings at the 10th percentile in the United States are less than half (47.4 percent) of those of the typical worker. This is the lowest share and is far below the (unweighted) peer average of 62.0 percent.

Earners at the 10th percentile in the United States are further from the U.S. median than 10th-percentile earners in peer countries are from their own countries' respective medians. However, median earnings vary across countries. Thus, the data do not directly tell us how well-off workers at the 10th percentile in other countries are compared with U.S. workers at the 10th percentile. . . .

Despite the relatively high earnings at the top of the U.S. income scale (as illustrated in *The State of Working America, 12th Edition*), inequality in the United States is so severe that low-earning U.S. workers are actually worse off than low-earning workers in all but seven peer countries. The United States ranks 12th out of the 19 peer countries shown.

Among the peer countries, the United States' tax and transfer system does the least to reduce the poverty rate.

International Comparisons

Turning to an international comparison of poverty rates, we examine the share of the population living below half the median household income in the United States and select OECD countries, a measure known as the relative poverty rate.

In the late 2000s, 17.3 percent of the U.S. population lived in poverty—the highest relative poverty rate among OECD peers. The U.S. relative poverty rate was nearly three times higher than that of Denmark, which had the lowest rate (6.1 percent), and about 1.8 times higher than the (unweighted) peer country average of 9.6 percent.

While the overall relative poverty rate in the United States is higher than that of peer countries, the extent of child poverty is even more severe. In 2009, the United States had the highest rate of child poverty among peer countries, at 23.1 percent—meaning that more than one in five children in the United States lived in poverty (as measured by the share of children living in households with household income below half of median household income). This level is almost five times as high as that of Iceland, which had the lowest level, at

4.7 percent, and over two times higher than the (unweighted) peer-country average of 9.8 percent.

Another useful way to look at the extent of child poverty in the United States relative to other countries is to examine the child poverty gap: the distance between the poverty line (defined here as half of median household income) and the median household income of children below the poverty line, expressed as a percentage of the poverty line. A smaller value means that the median household income of children below the poverty line is relatively close to the poverty line, while a larger number means their median income is further below the poverty line, i.e., that they are relatively more poor. The child poverty gap in the United States is 37.5 percent, the highest among peer countries. Therefore, not only is the incidence of child poverty greater in the United States, but U.S. children living in poverty also face higher relative deprivation than impoverished children in other developed countries.

Resource Allocation

To show how taxes and transfer income affect poverty rates, we can compare poverty rates based on income calculations that include taxes and government transfers with rates based on income calculations that exclude them ("pretax and transfer" poverty rates). While differences in the latter can be attributed to differences in market outcomes (such as the domestic economy but also a country's minimum wage, level of unionization, and other labor market institutions), the former reflects both market outcomes and variations in the extent of tax and transfer programs for low-income households. Differences between the two poverty rates are solely due to the government safety net. . . .

For example, the pretax and transfer poverty rate in the United States in the late 2000s was 27.0 percent, while the post-tax and transfer rate was 17.3 percent. The difference, 9.7 percentage points, is how much the U.S. tax and transfer system reduced the poverty rate. Among the peer countries, the United States' tax and transfer system does the least to reduce the poverty rate. In contrast, tax and transfer programs reduced the poverty rate in France by 25.4 percentage points (from 32.6 percent to 7.2 percent post tax and transfer). France's redistributive programs lowered poverty by about 2.5 times as much as those of the United States. The (unweighted) average effect of peer countries' tax and transfer programs is a poverty-rate reduction of 17.4 percentage points—an effect nearly two times greater than that produced by such programs in the United States. . . .

Factoring in Social Services Spending

Total social expenditure as a share of GDP for the United States and select OECD countries plotted against their post-tax and transfer poverty rates, provid[e] a clear picture of the relationship between social spending and poverty. Of these countries, the United States stands out as the country with the highest poverty rate and one of the lowest levels of social expenditure—16.2 percent of GDP, well below the vast majority of peer countries, which average 21.3 percent (unweighted). The figure suggests that relatively low social expenditures are at least partially implicated in the high U.S. poverty rate.

Peer countries are much more likely than the United States to step in where markets and labor policy fail in order to lift their most disadvantaged citizens out of poverty.

10

The Government Should Do More to Reduce Poverty

John Yarmuth

John Yarmuth is a Democratic congressman representing Kentucky's 3rd District.

When it comes to the government's role in addressing poverty, modern-day Republicans have badly strayed from the party's roots as a champion of the poor in the era of Abraham Lincoln. Congressional leaders must realize the importance of protecting the social safety net, which benefits not just individuals but all of America as it contributes to economic stability. Congress should also raise the minimum wage and increase opportunities for both businesses and workers by investing in public works infrastructure improvement projects, which could employ tens of thousands. The government must also reinvest in American education so people are ready to compete in today's highly skilled job market instead of being trapped in poverty.

In 1854, Abraham Lincoln wrote that the "object of government is to do for a community of people whatever they need to have done, but cannot do at all, or cannot so well do, for themselves, in their separate and individual capacities." Lincoln believed, in other words, that government is how we organize our responsibilities to each other.

Today, Republicans have a different view. After four years of a GOP [Grand Old Party/Republican] House slashing the social safety net, millions of Americans are going without, and Congress finds itself at a crossroads.

We could continue down the path guided by a small-government-at-any-cost ideology that would further reduce commitments to our basic responsibilities and accelerate established cycles of poverty. Or we can return to the path envisioned by President Lincoln, where government naturally assumes a smaller role—not by refusing to meet its responsibilities, but because in meeting those responsibilities fully, the need for government diminishes.

If we expect to have any hope of reducing poverty in generations to come, we need a strong safety net today.

Taking responsible steps to reduce poverty is not merely a moral imperative but an economic one. And Congress should act now.

First, we must protect our social safety net. This is not only crucial for those who require assistance—many of whom are full-time workers, children, seniors, disabled Americans, and veterans—but for our economy as a whole. Federal assistance helps millions of Americans escape poverty every year by providing the stability needed to take advantage of new opportunities. In fact, it is our safety net that allows full participation in the economy. More Americans purchasing goods means more Americans making them, which means more American jobs.

An Agenda of Opportunity

Yet 69 percent of the cuts in the Republicans' budget come from our safety net—including Medicaid [the government's health insurance program for the poor], nutrition assistance, and housing—while it ends the Medicare [the government's health insurance program for seniors] guarantee and raises prescription drug costs for seniors. If we expect to have any hope of reducing poverty in generations to come, we need a strong safety net today.

Second, we must pursue an agenda of opportunity for workers today and in the future. The minimum wage should be a living wage. Contrary to the myth, more than two-thirds of minimum-wage workers are adults, and one in four is raising children. Currently, minimum-wage workers earn $15,080 a year for full-time work—36 percent below the poverty level. To make ends meet, many rely on taxpayer assistance—more than $3,800 per fast-food employee each year, according to the National Employment Law Project. That's $1.2 billion annually in government assistance to McDonald's employees alone.

A higher minimum wage will immediately reduce dependence on public assistance, increase the spending power of millions of American consumers, and help workers take the steps necessary to break the cycle of poverty.

Investing in America

Third, Congress must help create an environment where businesses and workers can grow and thrive. This means long overdue infrastructure investments in roads, bridges, water systems, and grids—which will create tens of thousands of jobs immediately. But it also means investing in our human capital by making education accessible for every American and ensuring each is ready for the jobs of the future through training programs that focus on high-demand fields.

Each of these three steps relies on a principle that has been proven time and again throughout our nation's 238 years: An investment in Americans is an investment in America.

President Lincoln couldn't have envisioned the complex problems we face now. But when he wrote that government "embraces all which, in its nature, and without wrong, requires combined action, as public roads and highways, public schools, charities, pauperism, orphanage, estates of the deceased, and the machinery of government itself," he had a good handle on what it meant to use government as a tool to provide the stability and opportunity needed to attack poverty.

We don't call it pauperism anymore, but what Lincoln wrote applies in our time as much as it did in his own.

11

Government Programs Are Not the Solution to Poverty

Max Eternity

Max Eternity is an artist, writer, historian, and the founder of the Eternity Group, a global media company that focuses on independent news, reviews, food, art, and design.

Efforts to reform America's welfare system have failed and instead of lifting people out of poverty they have trapped poor people in a brutal and self-perpetuating system. Making even temporary welfare aid dependent on participating in the workforce amounts to punishment for those who cannot do so because of their circumstances, such as being a single mother without childcare resources. The poorest of the poor have been especially hard hit by welfare regulations that ultimately guarantee the spread and continuation of poverty. Government programs are not the answer to poverty in America; more meaningful progress could be made by working toward economic justice outside of the political framework of Washington, DC.

Whether by default or conscious implementation, a variety of institutional policies contribute to ongoing poverty. These include federal policies around poverty assistance and student debt, institutional barriers to upward social mobility and criminalization of poverty.

[Civil rights leader] Dr. Martin Luther King, Jr. once noted, "An edifice that produces beggars needs restructuring." However, though "beggars" are constantly being "produced" in every corner of the country, it is sometimes difficult to determine what the specific edifices that produce them look like, and where they lie. The politics and policies that create paradigms of poverty are often remote and administered with a hidden hand.

Facts and figures on the subject of poverty must be parsed: There are "beggars" living paycheck-to-paycheck, a step away from slipping into poverty. There are "beggars" mired in deep poverty, handed down generationally. And there are those in even deeper poverty, faced with homelessness and starvation.

Across the US government, most programs intended to eradicate poverty have served only to perpetuate it.

In 2011, according to a US Census Bureau report, the official poverty rate in the United States was 15 percent, amounting to 46.2 million people in poverty. The poverty rate for children under 18 was even more sobering, with more than one in five kids living in poverty.

Further, the numbers indicate that things have gotten worse over the past decade: Poverty hit a 17-year high in 2010, and remained at that rate in 2011. Rates are substantially worse for blacks and Latinos, more than a quarter of whom live in poverty.

It's clear that the edifice—the socioeconomic and political framework that drives these trends—has failed. But what would a true restructuring look like?

Federal Poverty Programs Do Not Lift the Poor Out of Poverty

Across the US government, most programs intended to eradicate poverty have served only to perpetuate it.

Sixteen years ago, President [Bill] Clinton signed off on a piece of welfare reform legislation called the Personal Responsibility and Work Opportunity Reconciliation Act (PRWOR), which bore the colloquial nomenclature "welfare to work." The Department of Health and Human Services web site states that PRWOR welfare recipients were required to "work in exchange for time-limited assistance." Clinton's welfare-to-work program also included "comprehensive child support enforcement" that claimed to be "the most sweeping crackdown on non-paying parents in history." Clinton's PRWOR welfare-to-work program is now called Temporary Assistance to Needy Families (TANF).

The underlying principle of the welfare-to-work approach inevitably tosses some of the neediest people to the sidelines.

For a short while in the late 1990s, the program did appear to reduce poverty. Whatever successes may have been achieved, however, were short-lived, according to a recent report from the Center on Budget and Policy Priorities (CBPP):

> Over the last 16 years, the national TANF caseload has declined by 60 percent, even as poverty and deep poverty have worsened. While the official poverty rate among families declined in the early years of welfare reform, when the economy was booming and unemployment was extremely low, it started increasing in 2000 and now exceeds its 1996 level.

> These opposing trends—TANF caseloads going down while poverty is going up—mean that a much smaller share of poor families receive cash assistance from TANF than they did prior to welfare reform.

According to Arloc Sherman, a senior researcher at CBPP, TANF has hastened a restructuring that ultimately exacerbated conditions for the poorest people. "It was about cutting different groups of people; for example, immigrants were cut from food stamps," he told *Truthout*.

A Weakening Safety Net

Sherman noted that "welfare to work" programs have, in some cases, helped folks living just below the poverty line to climb above it. However, he said, the change in structure "very much created a sink-or-swim world."

"The number of children and parents who fell below (the poverty line) increased by more than a million in the ensuing decade, and that is very directly tied to the weakening of the safety net for families who happened to be without work," Sherman said, adding that the programs proved to be "a real weakening of the safety net for those at the bottom, in deep poverty."

He added that the difficult economic climate of recent years has compounded these effects: When there's little work available, the "welfare-to-work" approach falls flat.

Though changes could likely be made to make TANF more just, the underlying principle of the welfare-to-work approach inevitably tosses some of the neediest people to the sidelines: Making aid contingent on a particular (sometimes impossible) involvement with the work force means that many people for whom that specific participation is not viable (many of them single mothers) simply "fall" off the rolls.

In a piece in *In These Times*, reporter Michelle Chen attributes worsening poverty to the "cruel" welfare-to-work policies of both Republicans and Democrats.

"[B]oth parties have gutted the welfare system as a whole to conduct a cruel social experiment on impoverished families," she states, adding that welfare "reform" amounts to a "punitive approach to poverty [that] has driven poor mothers of color further to the margins of the economy, making them even more politically invisible."

There Are No Policies to Increase Social Mobility

The ideal of "the American dream" has been slipping away quickly, even for those who aren't living in poverty. According to a recent Federal Reserve survey cited in *The New York Times*, "The median American family's net worth dropped by nearly 40 percent from 2007 to 2010—from $126,400 to $77,300—wiping out 18 years' worth of accumulated wealth." Perhaps it is this kind of data that led even financial self-help guru Suze Orman to declare in a 2010 *Forbes* magazine article, "The American dream is dead."

In an October 2012 story in *Der Spiegel*, Nobel Prize-winning economist Joseph Stiglitz echoed Orman, saying, "The American dream has become a myth." Stiglitz, former chief economist to the World Bank, continued: "There has been no improvement in well-being for the typical American family for 20 years. On the other side, the top one percent of the population gets 40% more in one week than the bottom fifth receive in a full year. In short, we have become a divided society. America has created a marvelous economic machine, but most of the benefits have gone to the top."

Changes in tax policies have allowed an elite few to escape the forces of gravity in terms of wealth and income.

The Declining Middle Class

The ongoing loss of the middle class in inner cities further evidences the fact that current policies favor a wealthy few, resulting in the return of once-modestly-integrated cities to near apartheid-like economic segregation. In the *San Francisco Chronicle*, Tyche Hendricks wrote in 2006, "The gentrification of San Francisco's neighborhoods reflects one facet of a national trend: the decline of middle-income neighborhoods in metropolitan America."

The acceleration of economic inequity and social immobilization is not an artifact of nature or natural forces; like poverty itself, it stems from the powerful "edifice" King describes.

Changes in tax policies have allowed an elite few to escape the forces of gravity in terms of wealth and income, permitting large corporations to escape taxes almost altogether. A parallel trend is also seen in trade policy, where a failure to enforce antitrust laws and unregulated finance has promulgated business models that undermine the viability of the independent small- to medium-size businesses that were once the bedrock of communal prosperity across America. These conjoined policies have also resulted in the creation of lower paying "McJobs", increasing the ranks of the working poor.

The Weight of Personal Debt

Changes in bankruptcy laws over the last 20 years have made it harder to declare personal bankruptcy and to escape certain kinds of debts—discouraging entrepreneurs and students, and condemning many people to perpetual debt servitude. This punitive personal debt, in fact, is a crucial, often downplayed issue in the landscape of economic injustice, according to economist Dean Baker, co-founder of the Center For Economic Policy and Research (CEPR) and regular *Truthout* contributor.

"[T]here were never very many people who made a successful run with a small business," Baker told *Truthout*. "The vast majority fail. . . . The bigger issue here is the new [(George) Bush administration] bankruptcy laws, which leave many people in debt for decades."

Other government policies that reduce access to education—once the great driver of social mobility—make the prospect of escaping from poverty even more difficult.

A case in point: The University of California (UC), California State University (CSU) and California Community Colleges (CCC) are the primary systems that constitute the (public) higher education system for the State of California. These systems used to receive far more state funding than did correctional facilities (prisons). However, higher education now receives slightly less funding than California's prison system.

This shift in both state and federal policies is traceable through the shift in budgetary priorities. Instead of providing the poor with an opportunity to learn their way out of poverty, the poor are being offered to the prison-industrial complex as commodities: When it comes to education funding in impoverished neighborhoods, "security" measures often take precedence over teaching and learning.

As the need for student loans has steadily increased, so has the number of borrowers who have fallen behind on making payments.

The Role of Education

"From metal detectors to drug tests, from increased policing to all-seeing electronic surveillance, the public school of the twenty-first century reflects a society that has become fixated on crime, security and violence," Annette Fuentes wrote in her book, *Lockdown High: When the Schoolhouse Becomes a Jailhouse*, published last year [2012]. In an interview with me last year, Fuentes commented on how the current public education system is failing America's youth—especially kids of color—in achieving a better life:

> It's clear that kids from certain demographics, including income, background, race and ethnicity, that we can look at that and predict how good the schools are, and rate of racial suspensions and zero tolerance policies. Part of that demographic is income, so when you look at that indicator that means that all those kids that come from the poverty level, generally speaking, can determine a kid's prospects in school; determine dropout rates and incidents with the criminal justice system. We know that African-American students will face a disproportionate experience with zero tolerance policies. These kids are more likely to drop out. It's like a daisy chain of circumstances that relate to a kid's background.

The problem of educational access overlaps with the personal debt debacle: As the need for student loans has steadily increased, so has the number of borrowers who have fallen behind on making payments. According to *The New York Times*, "Nearly one in every six borrowers with a loan balance is in default." This is a number "greater than the yearly tuition bill for all students at public two- and four-year colleges and universities."

More and more loans have become necessary to finance a higher education, as Pell grants and other government sources of funding for lower-income students have decreased—and as states, including California where the public higher education system was once a public pride and glory—have significantly reduced funding to universities. Meanwhile, debt relief options are increasingly scarce: Dean Baker [of CEPR] pointed to "the tightening of rules on relieving student loan debt" as one of the most important factors contributing to the widespread personal debt dilemma.

When the costs of incarceration are so high, reducing the corrections budget and reinvesting significantly in rehabilitation programs can still save states considerable money.

Break the Chains of Poverty

When viewed exclusively through a capitalistic lens, poverty may seem an individual failing instead of a systemic ill: Capitalists have long promulgated the idea that the poor are undeserving, lazy, morally inadequate. The governmental policies we've deconstructed—policies that assure the continuation and proliferation of poverty—tacitly (or, sometimes, straightforwardly) endorse this view. However, as we critique these policies, we must also highlight the many efforts directed toward true economic justice that have sprung up around the country in recent years: Grassroots organizations are finding alternative ways to combat poverty outside of the politics of lobbying the government. One inspiring example is the Ella Baker Center (EBC) in Oakland, California.

The Center, named for Ella Jo Baker, an "unsung hero of the civil rights movement," works through service and advocacy to combat poverty and confront the unjust "justice" system that criminalizes poor people.

Shifting Priorities

According to EBC's website, California's Division of Juvenile Justice has "an 81 percent recidivism rate and a cost of over $200,000 per youth, per year." I asked Jennifer Kim, EBC's senior policy analyst, how the funds could be better spent on poor, disenfranchised youth, in ways that might have a long-lasting impact.

"When the state spends $200,000 to lock up a youth in a broken system, it's a divestment away from creating opportunities and lifting up impoverished communities," Kim said, speaking specifically of California. "Other states have provided real rehabilitation programs that not only improve youth outcomes but they do it at a fraction of the cost."

When the costs of incarceration are so high, reducing the corrections budget and reinvesting significantly in rehabilitation programs can still save states considerable money, making it an attractive option for all groups involved, according to Kim.

"In a time where we have to tighten our budgets and figure out innovative ways to serve communities, it's helpful to know that other states are doing it, and they are doing it well," Kim said. "Instead of cutting health and human services or education that provide vital services, we should look at our bloated corrections budget, figure out what's not working, cut it out or close it down, and invest in alternatives that enhance public safety, improve outcomes—all at a savings."

Innovative advocacy groups are increasingly questioning—and pushing back against—the "welfare" programs that have entrenched the cycle of poverty. It remains to be seen whether, over the coming years, policymakers will begin to see the writing on the wall.

12

Economic Inequality Promotes Poverty

Lawrence Davidson

Lawrence Davidson is a history professor at West Chester University in Pennsylvania. He is the author of Foreign Policy Inc.: Privatizing America's National Interest *and other books.*

Poverty in the United States is not caused by the moral failures of poor people themselves; it is a structural problem that is a by-product of free-market capitalism, a system that generates extreme economic inequality. While the rich get richer in the United States, the poor necessarily get poorer, and they also become disadvantaged in other important ways, such as with diminished cognitive abilities. Lawmakers should take all of this into account as they craft public policies on welfare, but they stubbornly do not. Addressing the causes of the country's deep economic disparities and working to reverse them is a moral imperative for society; it will take bold action by the masses to force politicians into responsible action on poverty.

Most of the poverty in the United States is artificially manufactured. It is poverty created in the pursuit of "free market ideals," expressed in recent times by the imposition of neoliberal economic policies—the sort of policies that cut taxes on the wealthy, do away with fiscal and other business regulations, shred the social safety net, and erode middle-class stability—all while singing the praises of self-reliance and individual responsibility.

As a result we have done very well in making the rich richer and the poor both poorer and more numerous.

How many poor people are there in the United States? According to Current Population Survey (CPS), which puts out the government's official figures, as of 2012 about 15 percent of the population, or some 46.5 million people, were living in poverty. The rate for children under 18 comes in higher, at about 21.8 percent.

The U.S. government measures poverty in monetary terms. In 2012 poverty was defined as yearly total income of $23,050 or less for a family of four. The figure is adjusted for individuals or other size families.

Our economic system is condemning at least 48.5 million people to high rates of un- or underemployment . . . and all the other vicissitudes typically associated with a life of poverty.

Then there is the depressing fact that "most Americans (58.5 percent) will spend at least one year below the poverty line at some point between the ages of 25 and 75."

There happens to be more than one level to this economic version of hell, and so we should take note of the category of "deep poverty." Deep poverty is defined as having an income that is 50 percent of the official poverty level. This part of the population is growing.

In my area, which takes in southeast Pennsylvania and southern New Jersey, the percentage in deep poverty runs from 5 to 19 percent, depending on the county. These are people who, according to social service and charity workers, "have given up hope" and "given up on finding jobs."

Free-Market Consequences

Consider what all this really means. Our economic system is condemning at least 48.5 million people to high rates of un- or underemployment, poor performance in school and at work (when it is available), poor nutrition and eating habits, high instances of drug abuse, high crime rates, homelessness, high rates of preventable diseases, shorter life-spans, and all the other vicissitudes typically associated with a life of poverty.

Yet neoliberals and their allies would say none of this is society's fault or responsibility, rather it is the fault of the individual who, living in a "free" economic environment, makes his or her own choices and then must live with the consequences.

Well, that is one particularly inhumane way of looking at the situation. However, we have proof from relatively recent U.S. history that poverty can be ameliorated through government action without seriously disrupting "market choice."

Back in the mid-1960s millions of citizens marched on Washington for "jobs and freedom," and President Lyndon Johnson responded with his War on Poverty programs. Those programs reduced poverty significantly and did so without transforming the U.S. into a socialist republic. Unfortunately, this momentum was not to last.

Two things brought it to a crashing halt: a murderous war in Vietnam and the tragically wrongheaded neoliberal economic policies mentioned above. We are still stuck in this rut. We are still at war (though now it is in the Middle East) and our economic policies continue to be self-destructive.

Cognitive Dysfunction Is a Side Effect of Poverty

The neoliberal outlook is demonstrably wrong in a significant way. The notion that the poor can make "free and rational choices" and thus can be held responsible for their situation is incorrect. There is accumulating evidence that poverty literally "messes with your mind" in a way that obstructs responsible choices.

What living in poverty does is to hit a person with a toxic cocktail of overwhelming problems day in and day out.

In fact, the "free market" contributes to an environment that makes the poor decidedly unfree: confused, preoccupied, and feeling overwhelmed and hopeless. In other words, being poor makes you cognitively dysfunctional.

The latest research to show this was published in August 2013 in the journal *Science* and is titled "Poverty Impedes Cognitive Function." The gist of the argument is, "Poverty captures attention, triggers intrusive thoughts, and reduces cognitive resources." In other words, the more preoccupied one is with troubles, the less able one is to muster the "cognitive resources" necessary to rationally "guide choice and action."

Most people find themselves overwhelmed with problems now and then, but not constantly. What living in poverty does is to hit a person with a toxic cocktail of overwhelming problems day in and day out: financial problems, health problems, parenting issues, victimization by criminals and others, and the problem of just finding and keeping a job.

The authors also point out that the IQ difference between those living in poverty and those living above the poverty line can be as high as 13 points. This difference is not a function of genetics or race. It is created by the environment of poverty itself.

Upending Assumptions

This study is political dynamite. It lends support to the assertion that as long as neoliberal economics claims our allegiance, we will continue to condemn tens of millions of our citizens to a life not only of want, but also of high anxiety and poor cognitive ability. This puts the lie to the popular myth that the poor are disadvantaged because most of them are congenitally lazy.

It likewise challenges the conclusions of such works as Richard Herrnstein and Charles Murray's *The Bell Curve,* which attributed at least part of the statistical difference in intellectual performance between American blacks and white to genetics. In truth, whatever statistical difference there is does not reflect inherent intellectual ability so much as high levels of long-term stress, which reduces a person's ability to develop and apply their cognitive strengths.

It is quite interesting how the authors of the *Science* article conclude their piece. As it turns out, they have chosen to sidestep the real implications of their own data. Thus, they tell us "this perspective has important policy implications. First, policy-makers should beware of imposing cognitive taxes on the poor."

Short of radical changes in our economic thinking, what the poor in the U.S. need is another "War on Poverty."

What does that mean? It means that policy-makers should try to reduce the number of forms the poor have to fill out, the number of "lengthy interviews" they have to experience, the number of "new rules" they have to "decipher," all of which "consume cognitive resources" that we now know the poor have less of than those who are better off.

A Moral Imperative

Also, policy-makers should time their demands on the poor for specific periods when they are best able to handle them, such as when they receive whatever periodic income that they do get and momentarily feel less monetary stress. These conclusions constitute a rather shocking anticlimactic letdown!

The authors have helped us see the enormous damage poverty does. In response society has a moral obligation to deal with more than forms and lengthy interviews. History tells us that we can do, and indeed have done, much better.

Short of radical changes in our economic thinking, what the poor in the U.S. need is another "War on Poverty." Indeed, the obligation is not just a moral one. There is a collective economic self-interest to minimize poverty for to do so will decrease income inequality, increase overall health, promote social stability and lessen crime. It will also promote consumption, which should make the capitalists among us happy.

Do our politicians understand any of this? Seems not. Just this week [November 2013] the House of Representatives voted to cut the Food Stamp program by some $40 billion. That is neoliberal economics in action and proof positive that ideology and prejudice are stronger than scientific research when it comes to policy formulation.

Is there a way to reverse this stupidity? Yes, but it will take mass action. It is time to consider replaying the 1960s and force the politicians to act responsibly despite themselves.

13

Increasing the Minimum Wage Would Help Reduce Poverty

Elise Gould

Elise Gould is director of health policy research at the Economic Policy Institute (EPI), a nonprofit liberal think tank that advocates for low-to-moderate-income families.

There used to be a strong statistical link between economic growth and falling poverty rates, but widening income disparities between the rich and poor in the United States have made that a thing of the past. Adjusted for inflation, the wages of American workers have been stagnant for decades and are now more than 25 percent below their real value in the 1960s. Raising the national minimum wage is critical to help offset such egregious labor market inequalities and reduce poverty. Additional measures should include strengthening worker protections, bolstering unions, reducing employer wage theft, and refining labor market practices around sick time and family leave.

Broad-based wage growth—if we can figure out how to achieve it—would dwarf the impact of nearly every other economic trend or policy in reducing poverty. Even in 2010, the bottom fifth of working age American households relied on wages for the majority (56%) of their income. When you add in all work-based income including wage-based tax credits, nearly 70% of income for low-income Americans is work-related. Yes, the targeted efforts to strengthen the safety net are well deserved. Programs such as food stamps (SNAP), unemployment insurance, and Social Security have helped reduce poverty over the last four decades. But market based poverty (or poverty measured using only income from wages) has been on the rise and the safety net has to work even harder to counterbalance the growing inequalities of the labor market.

There was once a strong statistical link between economic growth and poverty reduction, but rising inequality has severed it, and the results are deeply dispiriting. If the statistical link between economic growth and falling poverty that held before the mid-1970s had not been broken by rising inequality, then poverty, as the government measures it, would be virtually eradicated today. Furthermore, the impact of rising inequality is nearly five times more important in explaining poverty trends than family structure.

The decline in unionization over the last several decades has led to increases in wage inequality and a loss of bargaining power for workers.

As the Economic Policy Institute has documented in our paper launching the Raise America's Pay project, this rise in inequality is simply the flip side of nearly stagnant hourly wage growth for the vast majority of the American workforce in the three decades before the Great Recession. So how to reverse this wage-stagnation, especially for low-wage workers? Below is a list of proposals, all linked in their attempt to rebuild institutions that provide bargaining power to workers who have had it taken from them in recent decades.

The Real Value of Money

The minimum wage is currently more than 25% below its real value in the late 1960s. The Congressional Budget Office (CBO) reports that the Harkin-Miller bill to raise the minimum wage to $10.10 would cumulatively boost incomes of people below the federal poverty line by $5 billion. And this is probably too conservative; other academic research finds that the same bill would lift more than 4 million people out of poverty. Among those who would see a raise from the Harkin-Miller bill, 55% are women and 25% are women of color. Nearly one-in-five kids would see at least one parent get a raise.

Another key policy priority should be efforts to level the playing field for workers to organize and form unions. The decline in unionization over the last several decades has led to increases in wage inequality and a loss of bargaining power for workers. And this bargaining power loss is not confined to union members themselves—unions often set wage-standards for entire sectors. Importantly, the decline in unionization is not a natural, inevitable phenomenon or a result of workers no longer wanting unions. It is the result of a policy decision to allow growing employer aggressiveness to tilt the playing field against organizing drives.

Strength in Numbers

This policy choice is clear when one looks at the evidence. First, unionization has held up much better in the public sector where employers have less ability to fight organizing drives. Second, in 2007, the share of non-union workers who said they wanted to be represented by a union or similar organization reached an all-time high at over 50%. There is a growing wedge between the desire to organize and bargain collectively and workers' ability to do so. And, third, even the most obvious form of employer aggressiveness—the firing of workers who are trying to organize—has risen sharply in recent decades, according to the National Labor Relations Board.

The fact is that the decline of unions can explain approximately one-third of the growth of wage inequality among men and approximately one-fifth among women since the 1970s. This rising wage inequality is the key driver behind stagnant wages for workers at the bottom. When low-wage workers have been able to organize, unionization is associated with higher wages and benefits for many, including: food preparation workers, cashiers, cafeteria workers, child-care workers, cooks, housekeepers, and home-care aides.

The social safety net remains crucial for low-income working families in this country and also needs reforms.

Wage Theft Trouble

Reducing wage theft is also particularly important to low-wage workers. Wage theft occurs when employers withhold wages that are owed to a worker, for example by requiring workers to work off the clock or refusing to pay overtime. There is widespread evidence of these practices and more—from tipped workers not being paid their wages to Apple store employees being forced to stand in line after their shift while their bags are checked for merchandise. In nearly 9,000 investigations of the restaurant industry, the wage and hour division of the Department of Labor found that 83.8% of the shops investigated had wage and hour violations—underscoring the enforcement problems.

Millions of low- and moderate-wage workers have also seen slow wage growth because they are working overtime and not getting paid for it. This is because the real value of the salary threshold under which all salaried workers, regardless of their work duties, are covered by overtime provisions has been allowed to erode dramatically. Simply adjusting the threshold for inflation since 1975 would raise it to $984 per week (or $51,000 on an annual basis), from its current level of $455 ($24,000 annually). This simple adjustment would guarantee millions of additional workers time-and-a-half pay when they work more than 40 hours in a week.

More Policy Recommendations

Other labor market policies and practices, which, if changed, would increase the wages of low- and moderate-wage workers, include: the misclassification of employees, such as construction workers who are deemed independent contractors so that the employer doesn't have to pay for workers' compensation. Just-in-time scheduling occurs when employers schedule workers erratically and sporadically, and denies workers any regularity in their schedule or pay. Think about how difficult that is for working parents who need to support their families and also find child care, or for workers who need a second job to make ends meet. Finally, paid sick time, paid family medical leave, and flexible work hours, all would support workers and their families.

The social safety net remains crucial for low-income working families in this country and also needs reforms. Everything from shoring up SNAP to extending (EITC) [the Earned Income Tax Credit] to childless adults to expanding Medicaid [the government's health insurance program for the poor] to people in those states which refuse federal dollars. We also should have universal pre-K and affordable and high quality child care—we need to use every tool in our toolbox to give kids a chance of success, reducing inequality at the starting gate of kindergarten.

But, if we really care about children in our country, then we also need to raise the wages of parents working hard every day to lift their families out of poverty. We need to enforce the labor standards we have, update the ones that need it, and put power back in the hands of workers to bargain for better working conditions for themselves and their families.

14

How Minimum Wage Laws Increase Poverty

George Reisman

George Reisman is professor emeritus of economics at Pepperdine University in southern California and the author of Capitalism: A Treatise on Economics.

Raising the minimum wage would not help reduce poverty. In fact, it would have the opposite effect because it would victimize the country's lowest-skilled workers and make it more difficult for them to find employment for which they are qualified. Raising the minimum wage will make lower-end jobs more attractive to people with greater education and skills who may not have considered them before at a lower pay scale. Those better-skilled and educated workers will outcompete unskilled workers for jobs, further worsening the poverty of the least-skilled workers and forcing them out of the labor pool. Raising the minimum wage would create more poverty, not reduce it.

Raising the minimum wage is a formula for causing unemployment among the least-skilled members of society. The higher wages are, the higher costs of production are. The higher costs of production are, the higher prices are. The higher prices are, the smaller are the quantities of goods and services demanded and the number of workers employed in producing them. These are all propositions of elementary economics that you and the President should well know.

It is true that the wages of the workers who keep their jobs will be higher. They will enjoy the benefit of a government-created monopoly that excludes from the market the competition of those unemployed workers who are willing and able to work for less than what the monopolists receive.

The payment of the monopolists' higher wages will come at the expense of reduced expenditures for labor and capital goods elsewhere in the economic system, which must result in more unemployment.

Those who are unemployed elsewhere and who are relatively more skilled will displace workers of lesser skill, with the ultimate result of still more unemployment among the least-skilled members of society.

The higher the minimum wage is raised, the worse are the effects on poor people.

The unemployment directly and indirectly caused by raising the minimum wage will require additional government welfare spending and thus higher taxes and/or greater budget deficits to finance it.

Your and the President's policy is fundamentally anti-labor and anti-poor people. While it enriches those poor people who are given the status of government-protected monopolists, it impoverishes the rest of the economic system to a greater degree. It does this through the combination both of taking away an amount of wealth equal to the monopolists' gains, and of causing overall production to be less by an amount corresponding to the additional unemployment it creates. The rise in prices and taxes that results from raising the minimum wage both diminishes the gains of the monopolists and serves to create new and additional poor people, while worsening the poverty of those who become unemployed.

The Minimum Wage Hurts the Poor

Furthermore, the higher the minimum wage is raised, the worse are the effects on poor people. This is because, on the one hand, the resulting overall unemployment is greater, while, on the other hand, the protection a lower wage provides against competition from higher-paid workers is more and more eroded. At today's minimum wage of $7.25 per hour, workers earning that wage are secure against the competition of workers able to earn $8, $9, or $10 per hour. If the minimum wage is increased, as you and the President wish, to $10.10 per hour, and the jobs that presently pay $7.25 had to pay $10.10, then workers who previously would not have considered those jobs because of their ability to earn $8, $9, or $10 per hour will now consider them; many of them will have to consider them, because they will be unemployed. The effect is to expose the workers whose skills do not exceed a level corresponding to $7.25 per hour to the competition of better educated, more-skilled workers presently able to earn wage rates ranging from just above $7.25 to just below $10.10 per hour. The further effect could be that there will simply no longer be room in the economic system for the employment of minimally educated, low-skilled people.

The Standard of Living

Of course, the minimum-wage has been increased repeatedly over the years since it was first introduced, and there has continued to be at least some significant room for the employment of such workers. What has made this possible is the long periods in which the minimum wage was *not* increased. Continuous inflation of the money supply and the rise in the volume of spending and thus in wage rates and prices throughout the economic system progressively reduce the extent to which the minimum wage exceeds the wage that would prevail in its absence. The minimum wages of the 1930s and 1940s—25¢ an hour and 75¢ an hour—long ago became nullities. To reduce and ultimately eliminate the harm done by today's minimum wage, it needs to be left unchanged.

If your goal is to raise the wages specifically of the lowest-paid workers, you should strive to eliminate everything that limits employment in the better-paid occupations.

The standard of living is not raised by arbitrary laws and decrees imposing higher wage rates, but by the rise in the productivity of labor, which increases the supply of goods relative to the supply of labor and thus reduces prices relative to wage rates, and thereby allows prices to rise by less than wages when the quantity of money and volume of spending in the economic system increase.

If raising the standard of living of the average worker is your and the President's goal, you should abandon your efforts to raise the minimum wage. Instead, you should strive to eliminate all government policies that restrain the rise in the productivity of labor and thus in the buying power of wages.

Too Many Regulations

If your goal is to raise the wages specifically of the lowest-paid workers, you should strive to eliminate everything that limits employment in the better-paid occupations, most notably the forcible imposition of union pay scales, which operate as minimum wages for skilled and semi-skilled workers. In causing unemployment higher up the economic ladder, union scales serve to artificially increase the number of workers who must compete lower down on the economic ladder, including at the very bottom, where wages are lowest. To the extent that occupations higher up could absorb more labor, competitive pressure at the bottom would be reduced and wages there could rise as a result.

Abolishing or at least greatly liberalizing licensing legislation would work in the same way. To the extent that larger numbers of low-skilled workers could work in such lines as driving cabs, giving haircuts, or selling hot dogs from push carts, the effect would also be a reduction in competitive pressure at the bottom of the economic ladder and thus higher wages there.

The principle here is that we need to look to greater economic freedom, not greater government intervention, as the path to economic improvement for everyone, especially the poor.

15

Poverty Negatively Affects Mental Functioning

Evan Nesterak

Evan Nesterak is editor-in-chief at The Psych Report, *a non-profit, web-based magazine focusing on behavioral science.*

The experience of poverty exacts a toll far beyond economics. Researchers at Harvard and Princeton have found that the typical stresses of poverty compromise an individual's mental functioning so much that it makes it harder for them to make decisions, follow directions, and complete tasks. The so-called cognitive burden of poverty overloads a person's finite mental resources and significantly impedes cognitive ability. The research findings are important because they could help policymakers shape policies and procedures that take the cognitive effects of poverty into account so their efforts don't work against the people they are trying to help.

Nobody is perfect. At times we have difficulty managing our finances, we don't always take our medications as planned, and sometimes we don't perform up to par at work. However, research shows that people experience these problems to different degrees. Across financial strata, research reveals that the financially less well-off engage in these behaviors more often than those who are financially stable. These behaviors are particularly concerning, because, for those with limited financial resources, they can lead to poverty as well as perpetuate it.

In their article, "Poverty Impedes Cognitive Function," which appears in the latest issue of *Science*, University of Warwick Professor Anandi Mani and several other social scientists suggest poverty, and the ever-present concerns that come with it, places an undue burden on an individual's limited mental resources. Compared with those who are free from poverty, this burden leaves those in poverty with fewer cognitive resources with which to make choices and take action. Mani et al. write, the poor "are less capable not because of inherent traits, but because the very context of poverty imposes load and impedes cognitive capacity."

However, it is important to note that their explanation is not limited to the traditional populations of poverty, defined by a specific income level or ability to access basic human needs. The authors define poverty "broadly as the gap between one's needs and the resources available to fulfill them." That is, people in poverty are those who feel "poor," who feel they have less than they need.

In the present work, Mani et al. demonstrated the impact of poverty on cognitive resources in two very different populations, New Jersey shopping mall-goers and Indian sugar cane farmers. The research showed that although the financial wealth differs considerably between these two populations, the "poor" in each population experienced diminished cognitive ability as a result of the cognitive burden imposed by their respective levels of poverty.

The New Jersey Mall Study

In the first study, Mani et al. presented New Jersey mall-goers with four financial scenarios about which they had to make a hypothetical decision. The scenarios were designed to induce participants to think about their own personal financial concerns. One scenario went as follows:

"Your car is having some trouble and requires $X to be fixed. You can pay in full, take a loan, or take a chance and forego the service at the moment.... How would you go about making this decision?"

The authors found that in the "easy" condition ... both rich and poor participants performed the cognitive tasks equally well. However, in the "hard" condition ... poor participants performed significantly worse than rich participants.

Some participants were presented with "easy" scenarios (a $150 car repair), while others were presented with "hard" scenarios (a $1,500 car repair). After being presented with either four "easy" or four "hard" scenarios, researchers tested participants' cognitive function, using two metrics; Raven's Progressive Matrices, which measures "fluid intelligence" and is used in IQ tests, and a spatial compatibility task, which measures cognitive control.

For their analysis, the researchers divided participants into two groups, "rich" and "poor." They did so by computing the median effective household income, which takes into account total household income and number of people in the household. Participants whose effective household income landed above the calculated median were considered "rich," while those whose fell below were considered "poor."

The authors found that in the "easy" condition, when financial concerns were presumably low, both rich and poor participants performed the cognitive tasks equally well. However, in the "hard" condition, when financial concerns were more salient, poor participants performed significantly worse than rich participants. The authors suggest that the "hard" condition evoked greater financial concerns in poor participants, than it did in the rich, which left the poor with less mental resources for the cognitive tasks, and lead to diminished performance.

The Sugar Cane Farmer Study

Building upon these results, Mani et al. investigated how naturally occurring financial pressures, rather than lab-induced, can impact cognitive functioning. Mani et al. studied Indian sugar cane farmers who are paid for their crop once per year. These farmers have trouble smoothing their consumption over the year, and as a result experience periods of wealth (post-harvest) and periods of poverty (pre-harvest). Mani et al. used this context to understand how cognitive ability can change as a function of a naturally occurring financial cycle.

One of most immediate implications is that policies and programs designed to help alleviate poverty could be more effective by making resources for the poor more accessible and less cognitively taxing.

During the pre-harvest, farmers report greater financial concerns than during the post-harvest. This is evident by the number of items they pawned, and the likelihood they had taken out a loan. Similar to poor participants at the mall, Mani et al. predicted that during the pre-harvest, with financial concerns weighing on their mind, farmers would perform worse on the cognitive tasks than during the post-harvest period, when financial concerns were less pressing. It is important to note that there was no experimental manipulation in this study. Mani et al. simply measured the cognitive ability of farmers during the naturally occurring pre- and post-harvest periods. In this study, researchers again employed the Raven's test, but due to the limitations in the field replaced the spatial compatibility task with a numerical stroop test.

Significant Results from Both Studies

As expected, during the pre-harvest farmers performed worse on the cognitive tasks than did farmers during the post-harvest. Furthermore, this effect held after controlling for farmer nutrition, stress, amount of physical work, and potential learned effects from taking the cognitive tests twice. Likewise, many of the calendar effects that one would expect when studying the harvest cycle (weather or yearly festivals) do not apply to sugar cane farmers, as harvest dates are arbitrarily set by the sugar mills and are spread throughout the year. Thus, Mani et al. conclude that pre-harvest farmers, like poor New Jersey mall-goers, experienced a reduction in cognitive ability, because their cognitive resources were consumed by the financial concerns they faced at that time.

Across the two studies, it is important to note the magnitude of the drop in cognitive ability. The drop in performance observed in poor New Jersey mall-goers and pre-harvest sugar cane farmers, when they felt the pressure of poverty, was comparable to losing a full night's sleep or a 13 point drop in IQ.

These findings have significant implications for poverty-related policy. One of most immediate implications is that policies and programs designed to help alleviate poverty could be more effective by making resources for the poor more accessible and less cognitively taxing. The authors write, "Policymakers should beware of imposing cognitive taxes on the poor just as they avoid monetary taxes on the poor. Filling out long forms, preparing for a lengthy interview, deciphering new rules, or responding to complex incentives all consume cognitive resources." While few policies take cognitive demand into account, research shows that relatively simple interventions that reduce cognitive demand—reminders, help with forms and planning, and built in defaults—could be the difference between whether or not a program designed to help the poor works for or against the people it is trying to help.

The New Science of Scarcity

Co-authors of this study, Harvard Economics Professor Sendhil Mullainathan and Princeton Psychology Professor Eldar Shafir have written a new book on how mentally taxing situations, like poverty, can affect cognitive ability. The book, *Scarcity: Why Having Too Little Means So Much*, introduces the "new science of scarcity," and reveals a pervasive logic and pattern of behavior that can leave people always dealing with scarcity; "having less than you feel you need." Mullainathan and Shafir show this to be true for money, time, and companionship, among other human needs. In the introduction to their book, they write:

"Scarcity captures the mind. Just as the starving subjects had food on their mind, when we experience scarcity of any kind, we become absorbed by it. The mind orients automatically, powerfully, toward unfulfilled needs. For the hungry, that need is food. For the cash strapped it might be this month's rent payment; for the lonely, a lack of companionship. Scarcity is more than just the displeasure of having very little. It changes how we think. It imposes itself on our minds."

16

Poverty Industry Drives Memphis Economy

Ted Evanoff

Ted Evanoff is a staff writer for the Commercial Appeal *newspaper in Memphis, Tennessee.*

Serving America's poor has become an industry in and of itself, and in many cities it comprises a major piece of the local economy. Nationwide, billions of dollars in economic activity revolve around interacting with poor people. The nature of those transactions range from one extreme to the other. Some businesses blatantly exploit the poor, such as predatory payday lenders, check-cashing stores, and pawn shops, while others are more neutral, like thrift stores, rent-to-own operations, and bail bondsmen. Others still, like social service agencies, health-care providers, charities, and foundations, provide local jobs and deliver services that are paid for by infusions of federal, state, and private money. Poverty Inc. is thus a growing industry.

Thousands of jobs have vanished from Memphis [Tennessee] since the economy collapsed in 2008. Yet, the city hasn't dried up. One reason: the annual injection of billions of poverty dollars. Home to half of the region's 200,000 low-income households, Memphis ranks regularly among the nation's poorest metropolitan areas, making it fodder for national misery indexes. But less understood, and less visible, is a robust industry that has quietly grown up around the city's legions of poor.

Memphis' poverty industry pumps at least $5 billion a year—five times FedEx's annual local payroll—into the economy, according to a study by *The Commercial Appeal* and the University of Memphis [U of M].

Just as the city's logistics industry has swelled around 30,000-employee FedEx and Memphis International Airport, a loosely aligned network of employers—everything from charities to landlords to check-cashing companies—has grown into one of the city's vital economic engines.

Year after year, metropolitan Memphis ranks among the nation's poorest metro areas. . . . Yet, the poor are still able to sustain hundreds of shops, stores and offices.

While it is difficult to pinpoint the exact financial impact of Poverty Inc. on the city and county's $46 billion economy, the newspaper found that at an estimated $5.3 billion per year, it rivals the region's largest industries: transportation and logistics, health care, even government.

"There's a lot of economic activity that revolves around the billions of dollars of commerce associated with poor people," said University of Memphis economist John Gnuschke who participated in the newspaper's study.

Year after year, metropolitan Memphis ranks among the nation's poorest metro areas. It now has the highest poverty rate of any metro with more than 1 million residents. Yet, the poor are still able to sustain hundreds of shops, stores and offices. This is largely due to the social safety net.

Just over $3 billion flowed from Washington for the 100,000 least well-off households in Memphis in 2010. This tide of cash never diminishes the poverty rate, which is based on earned wages. But the aid is real money.

Part of the safety net of social programs in place for the jobless, retired, disabled and poor, the $3 billion gets spent, flowing throughout Memphis, mixing with underground cash, state aid and philanthropic donations.

Add up all this cash, and $5.39 billion circulated in 2010 alone, according to the newspaper's study, helping support more than 1,000 businesses ranging from free medical clinics and payday lenders to grocers and car dealers.

Even though wages for thousands of Memphis families fall below the poverty line, they are still consumers. They eke out just enough aid individually to get by. Collectively, the 100,000 households support a wide slice of the Memphis economy.

"A lot of people in this town are very good at getting ahead in a get-by world," said Ruby Bright, executive director of Women's Foundation for a Greater Memphis. "Poor people are strategists within the resources they have available."

Poverty Inc.

At a time when policy makers in Washington are talking about scaling back federal spending, *The Commercial Appeal* set out to figure what share of the poverty business ties directly to government aid.

The tide of cash helps support scores of businesses leasing acres of building space along the city's commercial corridors.

Examining reports and records from 2010, the review shows Washington accounts for 56 percent of the $5.39 billion. This does not include all federal grants, such as federal law enforcement funds or the $293 million in federal money going to Memphis City Schools. The newspaper study focused on cash outlays that directly sustain poor citizens. The study shows:

- State and federal government agencies disbursed about $3.58 billion in 2010 for the 100,000 least well-off families in the city. Washington's share: $3.02 billion, including safety net and social programs such as welfare, Social Security, Medicaid health care and Section 8 rent subsidies.

- Shops, stores, offices, foundations and charities—from pawn shops to health clinics—whose clients are largely poor account for another $782 million. Baptist Memorial Hospital, for example, provided $51.9 million worth of uncompensated care in its 2011 budget year.

- An estimated $768 million is off-the-books cash never reported to the Internal Revenue Service for everything from lawn and garden work to illicit drug sales. *The Commercial Appeal* estimated the number from economists' studies of the U.S. underground economy.

Besides the impoverished families, one of every three working Memphians earn just enough to get tax credits meant to lift them out of poverty. In 2010, nearly 103,000 city residents received $261.6 million in tax refunds related directly to these earned income tax credits.

The tide of cash helps support scores of businesses leasing acres of building space along the city's commercial corridors. Nearly 800 payday lenders, pawn shops, tax refund offices, rent-to-own stores, check cashiers, car-title lenders and bail bond offices operate across the city, according to a U of M analysis for *The Commercial Appeal*.

Washington's Role

Exactly how big is the poverty trade in Memphis compared to other sectors of the economy? That's hard to say.

The figures above double-count some of the money. Tax refunds, for example, get spent at pawn shops. Food stamps are used at dollar stores. What's clear is that Washington stands out as an economic driver. Take the two largest sources of federal money.

Safety net programs including food stamps and welfare contributed $1.2 billion in 2010 for the city's 100,000 poorest households. Medicaid disbursed $1.1 billion, including funds for some Memphians who are not classified as poor, such as disabled people.

While a tide of cash fuels the poverty trade in Memphis, the money barely dents the poverty rate.

If this $2.3 billion were a straight transfer of cash, it would equal 9.6 percent of all the wages and salaries paid in 2010 to every resident in the city and county.

Only four sectors top this: Government including public schools and colleges (22 percent of all salaries and wages in the city and county), logistics (17 percent), health care (16 percent), manufacturing (12.5 percent).

Even at 9.6 percent, the funding is considerable. FedEx, for example, is Memphis' largest company. Yet, the federal outlays dwarf its $1 billion-plus annual Memphis payroll.

Poverty Rate

While a tide of cash fuels the poverty trade in Memphis, the money barely dents the poverty rate.

Indeed, the tide has risen. And the poverty rate remains high. This traces in part to the recession wiping out jobs.

Presently, about 606,000 jobs are filled in the eight-county metro area, about the same level as in 1998. Poverty has increased as a result.

In its latest study, the U.S. Census reported 19.1 percent of the residents in metropolitan Memphis lived in poverty in 2011, a rate higher than the 50 other American metropolitan areas exceeding 1 million population.

As jobs vanished, the safety net expanded. Medicaid disbursements, for example, rose 62 percent between 2000 and 2010 in Memphis and Shelby County. Food stamps, now called the Supplemental Nutrition Assistance Program, quadrupled as the jobless rate climbed from 3.6 percent in 2000 to 11.1 percent in 2010.

None of this money reduced the official poverty rate. It is based on pretax household income reported on tax forms. A family of three that earns $19,090 in annual pretax wages is at the official poverty line regardless of how much rent subsidy, food stamps and other aid they get. Because the safety net money is not earned income, it is not counted in poverty rate calculations.

This has caused some experts to rethink how poverty should be defined. Basing a poverty measure on consumption provides a clearer look than a poverty rate based on earned income, say professors Bruce Meyer and James Sullivan. They research poverty at, respectively, the University of Chicago and the University of Notre Dame.

Across the nation, households with an annual income of less than $10,000 lived on average as if they had made $21,000, according to a consumption survey last year of 122,287 households in all income strata.

"Many of the major antipoverty initiatives of the last few decades are not reflected in the poverty rate, because policies like a rise in the Earned Income Tax Credit, a more generous Child Tax Credit, and expansions of Medicaid and food stamps do not show up as pretax money income," Meyer and Sullivan report in the *Journal of Economic Perspectives'* summer 2012 edition.

Spending Power

What they're saying is the poverty rate doesn't reflect actual living standards. What it means in Memphis is the poverty industry rolls along despite the rising poverty rate. Poor families still consume goods and services.

Across the nation, households with an annual income of less than $10,000 lived on average as if they had made $21,000, according to a consumption survey last year of 122,287 households in all income strata by the U.S. Bureau of Labor Statistics (BLS).

Government aid including welfare, food stamps, and rent subsidies accounted for the bulk of the $11,000 difference in the BLS survey. Off the books cash, the survey noted, averaged $1,100 per year, while annual Social Security payments added $2,800 per family.

Just as the safety net pumps cash into Memphis families, they in turn spend the money. Across the city, the workforce bulges where the poor and working poor make up a large share of the client base. For example:

Memphis and Shelby County contain a greater share of collection agency employees than the nation as a whole. Being above the national per capita rate adds 412 jobs and $14.1 million in payroll, according to a proportional analysis by *The Commercial Appeal* that uses U.S. Bureau of Economic Analysis data.

The system has it now where if someone has fallen, it's hard to get back up.

Grantsmaking, voluntary health and other charities employ one worker for every 2,369 residents in the United States. In Shelby County, the rate is one worker for every 884 residents. Being above the national rate adds $36 million in payroll here.

Payday lenders and check-cash shops average one employee per 2,013 residents in communities throughout the nation. Here, the rate is one employee per 530 residents, adding 464 jobs and $62.4 million in payroll.

Memphis Tides

In some neighborhoods, nearly 20 percent of the households report annual income of less than $10,000—enough to sustain some businesses.

"Our customers are really good people. They just don't have bank accounts. We're their bank," said Ann Agee-Gates, managing partner of Happy Hocker, a pawnshop on East Parkway.

Sustained by safety net programs, one unemployed single resident of South Memphis can survive. Add up the food stamps and her parent's rent subsidy and Social Security, and they live as if they earned $400 per week.

"I've put my life on hold. I've learned to live basically," said the woman, who asked not to be identified because she was embarrassed by life lived without a job. "The system has it now where if someone has fallen, it's hard to get back up."

She said she left the workforce recently to help her elderly parent in an emergency. She can now return to work. The parent is stable. But she's just comfortable enough to stay home, she said, especially when good wages seem hard to find in a region with a current 8.6 percent unemployment rate.

She lives in the parent's apartment. Medicaid and Social Security checks cover the parent's basics. Energy is used sparingly to keep the monthly bill under $150. Rent costs the two of them less than $150 per month after the Section 8 subsidy payment. The daughter contributes about $200 per month worth of food stamps.

"Food stamps make me able to live almost at a standstill," she said. "It plagues me that I'm not working. I know I have to get work some day. But right now I don't have to."

Her tax refund exceeded $1,000 including an Earned Income Tax Credit spent long ago, she said. She figures pawned jewelry, watches and clothes will bring in another $1,000. She makes about $100 each month or so doing odd jobs.

"I've lived where I was able to be frivolous," she said. "I wish I had thought to save. Now, whatever I get goes into our home. I'm going to turn this around. I just have to trust in God."

Although 96,000 households here rarely or never use banks, economic life hasn't disappeared, not with a $5.39 billion tide of money flowing across the city. Poor isn't the same as destitute.

Organizations to Contact

The editors have compiled the following list of organizations concerned with the issues debated in this book. The descriptions are derived from materials provided by the organizations. All have publications or information available for interested readers. The list was compiled on the date of publication of the present volume; names, addresses, phone and fax numbers, and e-mail and Internet addresses may change. Be aware that many organizations take several weeks or longer to respond to inquiries, so allow as much time as possible.

American Enterprise Institute for Public Policy Research (AEI)
1150 17th St. NW, Washington, DC   20036
(202) 862-5800 • fax: (202) 862-7177
website: www.aei.org

The American Enterprise Institute is an independent, non-profit research organization associated with the neoconservative movement in American foreign policy and Republican administrations since the 1980s. AEI scholars advocate limited government, tax reduction, capitalist enterprise, and individual responsibility as the best responses to poverty. The AEI website offers an archive of op-eds, newsletters, position papers, government testimony, and longer monographs on poverty-related topics such as welfare and health insurance reform, as well as the daily online business magazine, *The American*.

Benefits.gov
(800) 333-4636
website: www.benefits.gov

Sponsored by a partnership of federal agencies including all cabinet-level departments, the Social Security Administration, and the US Small Business Administration, Benefits.gov is the official benefits website of the US government, with the most comprehensive and up-to-date information on more than one thousand federal and state benefits and assistance programs for poor Americans. Searchable by state, the site explains eligibility requirements and provides links for food/nutrition (such as food stamps), education, housing, health care, and job-training programs.

Brookings Institution
1775 Massachusetts Ave. NW, Washington, DC   20036
(202) 797-6000 • fax: (202) 797-6004
e-mail: communications@brookings.edu
website: www.brookings.edu

The Brookings Institution, founded in 1927, is a liberal-centrist think tank whose fellows conduct research on and debate issues of foreign policy, economics, government, and the social sciences. Its scholars publish analyses of domestic and global antipoverty policy in the quarterly journal *Brookings Review* and in position papers such as "Immigration and Poverty in America's Suburbs" and "Fighting Poverty the American Way."

Cato Institute
1000 Massachusetts Ave. NW, Washington, DC   20001-5403
(202) 842-0200 • fax: (202) 842-3490
website: www.cato.org

The Cato Institute is a libertarian public policy research foundation dedicated to individual liberty, free markets, and limited government. It opposes, for example, minimum wage laws, trade barriers, and expansion of executive power, and supports noninterventionist foreign policy, a balanced federal budget, and workers' right to opt out of the Social Security program. It offers numerous publications on public policy, including the triannual *Cato Journal*, the bimonthly newsletter *Cato Policy Report*, and the quarterly magazine *Regulation*. Numerous poverty-related studies and position papers are available on the website.

Center for American Progress (CAP)

1333 H St. NW, 10th Floor, Washington, DC   20005
(202) 682-1611
website: www.americanprogress.org

The Center for American Progress is an independent, nonpartisan educational institute dedicated to improving the lives of Americans through progressive ideas and action. The organization conducts a wide variety of original research each year on topics such as poverty, the economy, education, health care, and other social issues and public policy matters. The CAP website features an extensive collection of news articles, issue briefs, fact sheets, and reports concerning poverty, including such recent publications as "The Top 10 Solutions to Shrink Poverty and Grow the Middle Class" and "Rep. Ryan's New Poverty Plan Is Not the Answer to the Pope's Prayers."

Center on Budget and Policy Priorities (CBPP)

820 First St. NE, Suite 510, Washington, DC   20002
(202) 408-1080 • fax: (202) 408-1056
e-mail: center@cbpp.org
website: www.cbpp.org

The Center on Budget and Policy Priorities is a nonprofit research and advocacy group that researches and represents the needs of low-income people in setting budget and tax policy. Founded in 1981 to analyze federal budget priorities, the center expanded its focus in the 1990s to funding for the poor at the state level (the State Fiscal Analysis Initiative) and in developing countries (the International Budget Project). CBPP maintains an online library of reports, statistics, slide shows, and analyses of the government's poverty and income data.

Children's Defense Fund (CDF)

25 E St. NW, Washington, DC   20001
(800) 233-1200
e-mail: cdfinfo@childrensdefense.org
website: www.childrensdefense.org

The Children's Defense Fund, founded in 1973, is a private, nonprofit organization that aims to ensure the health, education, and safety of all children. Led by founder and president Marian Wright Edelman, the fund lobbies legislators in support of Medicaid and the Children's Health Insurance Program (CHIP), the Head Start early education program, and other services for disadvantaged and poor children. Numerous publications are available for free download from the fund's website, including "A Portrait of Inequality" and fact sheets by state on child poverty, hunger, welfare, health, education, and at-risk youth.

Coalition on Human Needs (CHN)

1120 Connecticut Ave. NW, Suite 910, Washington, DC   20036
(202) 223-2532 • fax: (202) 223-2538
e-mail: jsandager@chn.org
website: www.chn.org

The Coalition on Human Needs is an alliance of national organizations working together to promote public policies that address the needs of low-income and other vulnerable people. CHN promotes adequate funding for human needs programs, progressive tax policies, and other federal measures to address the needs of low-income and other vulnerable populations. It publishes the *Human Needs Report* newsletter every other Friday when Congress is in session.

Economic Policy Institute (EPI)

1333 H St. NW, Suite 300, East Tower
Washington, DC   20005-4707
(202) 775-8810 • fax: (202) 775-0819
e-mail: epi@epi.org
website: www.epi.org

The Economic Policy Institute is a nonprofit, progressive think tank created in 1986 to represent the interests of low- and middle-income workers in the debate over US economic policy. It supports minimum wage laws and workers' right to form unions. Its fellows track trends in wages, benefits, union participation, and other economic indicators; testify before Congress and state legislatures; advise policymakers; and publish books, studies, and issue guides on poverty-related topics such as welfare, offshoring, and the living wage. EPI also produces the biennial *The State of Working America* and other reports.

Heritage Foundation

214 Massachusetts Ave. NE, Washington, DC   20002
(202) 546-4400 • fax: (202) 546-0904
e-mail: info@heritage.org
website: www.heritage.org

The Heritage Foundation is a conservative public policy research institute dedicated to "principles of free enterprise, limited government, individual freedom, traditional American values, and a strong national defense." Its resident scholars publish position papers on a wide range of complex issues in its *Backgrounder* series and in its quarterly journal *Policy Review*. Numerous poverty-related documents also are archived on the group's website, which additionally offers commentaries, podcasts, and a blog.

National Center for Children in Poverty (NCCP)

215 W 125th St., 3rd Floor, New York, NY   10027
(646) 284-9600 • fax: (646) 284-9623
e-mail: info@nccp.org
website: www.nccp.org

Based at Columbia University in New York, the National Center for Children in Poverty is a nonpartisan, public policy research center dedicated to promoting the economic security, health, and well-being of low-income families and children. The group's annual "Basic Facts About Low-Income Children" fact sheet series provides comprehensive information about children of different ages in the United States, and the NCCP website provides demographic and statistical analyses about the status of low-income children on a state-by-state basis. An interactive "Basic Needs Budget Calculator" on the site calculates how much money it takes for a family to afford minimum daily necessities in each state, and the calculator allows users to create customized results by changing assumptions about basic family expenses.

US Census Bureau
4600 Silver Hill Rd., Washington, DC   20233
(800) 923-8282
website: www.census.gov

The US Census Bureau is the official source of statistics on poverty in America. Its website sections cover how poverty is measured, definitions of poverty-related terms, up-to-date dollar amounts used to determine poverty status, poverty causes and projections, comparisons with poverty in foreign countries, and a Q&A section. Numerous reports and briefs available for download include the annual *Income, Poverty, and Health Insurance Coverage in the United States* and *The Effects of Taxes and Transfers on Income and Poverty in the United States*.

Bibliography

Books

Sasha Abramsky   *The American Way of Poverty: How the Other Half Still Lives*. New York: Nation, 2013.

Peter Edelman   *So Rich, So Poor: Why It's So Hard to End Poverty in America*. New York: New Press, 2012.

Barbara Ehrenreich   *Nickel and Dimed: On (Not) Getting By in America*, 10th ed. New York: Picador, 2011.

George Gilder   *Wealth and Poverty—A New Edition for the Twenty-First Century*. Washington, DC: Regnery, 2012.

John Iceland   *Poverty in America: A Handbook*. Berkeley, CA: University of California Press, 2013.

Woody Klein   *American Poverty: Presidential Failures and a Call to Action*. Washington, DC: Potomac, 2013.

Sandra Morgen, Joan Acker, and Jill Weigt   *Stretched Thin: Poor Families, Welfare Work, and Welfare Reform*. Ithaca, NY: Cornell University Press, 2009.

Sendhil Mullainathan and Eldar Shafir   *Scarcity: Why Having Too Little Means So Much*. New York: Times Books, 2013.

Nina Munk   *The Idealist: Jeffrey Sachs and the Quest to End Poverty*. New York: Doubleday, 2013.

Kathleen Pickering et al.	*Welfare Reform in Persistent Rural Poverty: Dreams, Disenchantments, and Diversity.* University Park, PA: Penn State University Press, 2011.
Stephen Pimpare	*A People's History of Poverty in America.* New York: New Press, 2008.
Gary Rivlin	*Broke, USA: From Pawnshops to Poverty, Inc.—How the Working Poor Became Big Business.* New York: HarperCollins, 2010.
Kristin S. Seefeldt and John D. Graham	*America's Poor and the Great Recession.* Bloomington, IN: Indiana University Press, 2013.

Periodicals and Internet Sources

Sasha Abramsky	"The Other America, 2012: Confronting the Poverty Epidemic," *Nation*, April 25, 2012.
Sasha Abramsky	"Why We Need a New War on Poverty," *Nation*, January 8, 2014.
Maryam Adamu	"Dignified Jobs and Decent Wages: The Next 50 Years of Civil Rights and Economic Justice," Center for American Progress, July 2014. www.americanprogress.org.
Karl Alexander and Linda Olson	"Urban Poverty, in Black and White," CNN, July 11, 2014. www.cnn.com.

Sylvia A. Allegretto and Steven C. Pitts	"To Work with Dignity: The Unfinished March Toward a Decent Minimum Wage," Economic Policy Institute, August 26, 2013. www.epi.org.
Emily Badger	"How Poverty Taxes the Brain," *City Lab*, August 29, 2013. www.citylab.com.
Dean Baker	"Poverty: The New Growth Industry in America," *Huffington Post*, August 29, 2012. www.huffingtonpost.com.
Pooja Bhatia	"A Tale of Two Cities: Mixing the Urban Poor Into a Rich Urban Life," National Public Radio, July 1, 2014. www.npr.org.
Josh Bivens et al.	"Raising America's Pay: Why It's Our Central Economic Policy Challenge," Economic Policy Institute, June 4, 2014. www.epi.org.
Elizabeth Blair	"In Confronting Poverty, 'Harvest of Shame' Reaped Praise and Criticism," National Public Radio, May 31, 2014. www.npr.org.
Charles M. Blow	"Paul Ryan, Culture and Poverty," *New York Times*, March 21, 2014.
Alyssa Brown	"With Poverty Comes Depression, More than Other Illnesses," Gallup, October 30, 2012. www.gallup.com.

Philip Bump   "The Source of Black Poverty Isn't
                     Black Culture, It's American Culture,"
                     Wire, April 1, 2014.
                     www.thewire.com.

Happy Carlock   "A Different Type of
                     Poverty—Journalist Sasha Abramsky
                     Looks at What It Means to Be Poor
                     in America," *U.S. News & World
                     Report*, September 5, 2013.

Zoë Carpenter   "Eighty-Six Percent of Americans
                     Think the Government Should Fight
                     Poverty," *Nation*, January 7, 2014.

James Cersonsky   "What a Real 'War on Poverty' Looks
                     Like," *Nation*, January 3, 2013.

Sally J. Clark   "Why Seattle Raised Our Minimum
                     Wage, and Why America Should
                     Too," CNN, June 3, 2014.
                     www.cnn.com.

Patricia Cohen   "'Culture of Poverty' Makes a
                     Comeback," *New York Times*, October
                     17, 2010.

Neal Conan   "Reconsidering the 'Culture Of
                     Poverty,'" *Talk of the Nation*, October
                     20, 2010. www.npr.org.

Matt Cover   "Study: More than Half a Trillion
                     Dollars Spent on Welfare but Poverty
                     Levels Unaffected," CNS News, June
                     25, 2012. http://cnsnews.com.

Sheldon Danziger and Christopher Wimer	"The Poverty and Inequality Report," Stanford Center on Poverty and Inequality, 2014. http://web.stanford.edu.
Drew Desilver	"Who's Poor in America? 50 Years into the 'War on Poverty,' a Data Portrait," Pew Research Center, January 13, 2014. www.pewresearch.org.
Jeffrey Dorfman	"The Minimum Wage Debate Should Be About Poverty Not Jobs," *Forbes*, February 22, 2014.
James A. Dorn	"Poor Choices," *Baltimore Sun*, September 27, 2011.
Elizabeth Drew	"The Republicans' War on the Poor," *Rolling Stone*, October 24, 2013.
Economist	"Towards the End of Poverty," June 1, 2013.
Peter Edelman	"The State of Poverty in America," *American Prospect*, June 22, 2012. http://prospect.org.
Peter Edelman	"Poverty in America: Why Can't We End It?" *New York Times*, July 28, 2012.
Thomas B. Edsall	"Making Money Off the Poor," *New York Times*, September 17, 2013.
Pam Fessler	"One Family's Story Shows How the Cycle of Poverty Is Hard to Break," National Public Radio, May 7, 2014. www.npr.org.

Pam Fessler   "The Changing Picture of Poverty:
                     Hard Work Is 'Just Not Enough,'"
                     National Public Radio, May 7, 2014.
                     www.npr.org.

Pam Fessler   "Rep. Ryan Unveils His Anti-Poverty
                     Plan, a Rebuke to LBJ Programs,"
                     National Public Radio, July 24, 2014.
                     www.npr.org.

Paul Gorski   "The Myth of the Culture of
                     Poverty," *Educational Leadership*,
                     April 2008. www.ascd.org.

Susan Greenbaum   "Debunking the Pathology of
                     Poverty," Aljazeera America, March
                     26, 2014.
                     http://america.aljazeera.com.

Terry Gross   "Turning Poverty into a
                     Multibillion-Dollar Industry," *Fresh
                     Air*, June 7, 2010. www.npr.org.

Ron Haskins   "To Tackle Poverty, We Need to
                     Focus on Personal Responsibility,"
                     New York Times, January 5, 2014.

Joshua Holland   "Think Tank Report Says Poor
                     Americans Have It Too Good,"
                     Moyers and Company, August 21,
                     2013. http://billmoyers.com.

Sally Kohn   "Exploiting Poverty Caused the
                     Financial Crisis," *Huffington Post*,
                     September 18, 2008.
                     www.huffingtonpost.com.

Paul Krugman	"On Fighting the Last War (on Poverty)," *New York Times*, January 8, 2014.
Helen F. Ladd and Edward B. Fiske	"Class Matters. Why Won't We Admit It?" *New York Times*, December 11, 2011.
Les Leopold	"America's Greatest Shame: Child Poverty Rises and Food Stamps Cut While Billionaires Boom," *Huffington Post*, November 8, 2013. www.huffingtonpost.com.
Leonard Lopate	"Strapped: A Look at Poverty in America," WNYC, 2014. www.wnyc.org.
Annie Lowrey	"House Budget Committee to Hold Hearing on Poverty," *New York Times*, April 30, 2014.
Jennifer Ludden	"To Break Cycle of Child Poverty, Teaching Mom and Dad to Get Along," National Public Radio, July 8, 2011. www.npr.org.
Lisa Mascaro	"Rep. Paul Ryan Calls for Cuts in Anti-Poverty Programs," *Los Angeles Times*, March 3, 2014.
National People's Action	"Profiting from Poverty: How Payday Lenders Strip Wealth from the Working Poor for Record Profits," January 2012. http://npa-us.org.

Pedro Noguera   "Bolder, Broader Strategy to Ending Poverty's Influence on Education," *Huffington Post*, December 2, 2011. www.huffingtonpost.com.

Toluse Olorunnipa and Elizabeth Campbell   "Ferguson Unrest Shows Poverty Grows Fastest in Suburbs," Bloomberg, August 18, 2014. www.bloomberg.com.

Jay Parini   "What Jesus Knew About Income Inequality," CNN, August 21, 2014. www.cnn.com.

Harold Pollack   "Being Poor Changes Your Thinking About Everything," *Washington Post*, September 13, 2013.

President's Council of Economic Advisers   "The War on Poverty 50 Years Later: A Progress Report," The White House, January 2014. www.whitehouse.gov.

Barbara Raab   "'Nursery School Dropouts': Poverty as a Health Crisis for Many of America's Kids," NBC News, September 6, 2013. www.nbcnews.com.

Len Ramirez   "San Jose Leaders Look to Build 'Pods,' 'Microhouses' to Shelter the Homeless," KCBS, April 29, 2014. http://sanfrancisco.cbslocal.com.

Robert Rector   "Strange Facts About America's 'Poor,'" *National Review Online*, September 13, 2011. www.nationalreview.com.

Gary Rivlin	"Fat Times for the Poverty Industry," *Atlantic*, June 9, 2010.
Gary Rivlin	"America's Poverty Tax," Daily Beast, September 8, 2011. www .thedailybeast.com.
Avik Roy	"On Labor Day 2013, Welfare Pays More than Minimum-Wage Work in 35 States," *Forbes*, September 2, 2013.
Joseph J. Sabia	"Minimum Wages: A Poor Way to Reduce Poverty," *Cato Tax and Budget Bulletin*, March 2014. www.cato.org.
Rachel Sheffield	"More Government Welfare Doesn't Equal Poverty Relief," *Daily Signal*, April 12, 2012. http://dailysignal.com.
Elizabeth Shell	"How the US Compares on Income Inequality and Poverty," PBS, June 19, 2014. www.pbs.org.
Matthew Spalding	"Why the US Has a Culture of Dependency," CNN, September 21, 2012. www.cnn.com.
Michael D. Tanner	"War on Poverty at 50—Despite Trillions Spent, Poverty Won," Cato Institute, January 8, 2014. www.cato.org.
Oliver Thomas	"A Poverty, Not Education, Crisis in US," *USA Today*, December 10, 2013.

Linda Walther
Tirado
"Why I Make Terrible Decisions, or,
Poverty Thoughts," *Huffington Post*,
October 22, 2013.
www.huffingtonpost.com.

US House of
Representatives
Budget
Committee
"The War on Poverty: 50 Years
Later," March 3, 2014.
http://budget.house.gov.

Sadhbh Walshe
"Banking While Poor: How Banks
Profit from Predatory Payday
Lending," *Guardian*, February 2013.

Hilary Wething
"Fixing the Gender Wage Gap Is a
Crucial Step for Women, but Not the
Only Step," Economic Policy
Institute, March 6, 2014.
www.epi.org.

Christopher
Wimer et al.
"Trends in Poverty with an Anchored
Supplemental Poverty Measure,"
Columbia Population Research
Center, December 5, 2013.
http://socialwork.columbia.edu.

World Hunger
Education Service
"Hunger in America: 2013 United
States Hunger and Poverty Facts,"
2013. www.worldhunger.org.

Tim Worstall
"If the US Spends $550 Billion on
Poverty How Can There Still Be
Poverty in the US?" *Forbes*,
September 9, 2012.

John Ydstie — "The Merits of Income Inequality: What's the Right Amount?" National Public Radio, May 18, 2014. www.npr.org.

Matthew Yglesias — "Bad Decisions Don't Make You Poor, Being Poor Makes for Bad Decisions," *Slate*, September 3, 2013. www.slate.com.

Index

W

Y